THROUGH SHADOWS INTO LIGHT

John Moloney,

Irish Messenger Publications
37 Lower Leeson Street, Dublin 2, Ireland

"The light shining in darkness is the token of true religion".

John Henry Newman

First Printing 1985

Imprimi Potest:
Coemgenus
Archbishop of Dublin
10 February 1985.

Nihil Obstat:
John Leonard, S.J.
Censor Deputatus,
10 February 1985.

© Irish Messenger Publications,
37 Lower Leeson Street, Dublin 2, Ireland.

ISBN 0 901335 41 X

Design: Carlos McCambridge.

Printed by The Nationalist, Carlow.

0005.

By the same author

No Greater Love
Pilgrims with Mary
Living the Mass
Bernadette Speaks
With Jesus to Calvary
Roads to his Heart

ACKNOWLEDGEMENT

The Scripture quotations in this publication
are from the Revised Standard Version of the
Bible Catholic Edition, copyrighted 1966 by the
Division of Christian Education of the National
Council of the Churches of Christ in the U.S.A.

Contents

Introduction

J ESUS loved his own until the end, and those who would respond to his love must also love him until the end. Love means following, not merely seeking the traces of his footsteps on the roads he trod, but following him with our hearts.

While every gospel page is a kind of epiphany through which shines some aspect of the wonders of his love, the Redeemer of man most vividly showed forth his redeeming love when he offered himself on the Cross for the redemption of the world. His whole life was directed towards that moment. ". . . He steadfastly set his face to go to Jerusalem." (Luke, 9, 51). With an intense desire he moved towards the dark night of his Passion and Death; and with equally intense joy he arose to give us a new world.

The Church lives by the Paschal Mystery. Through it she presents to us the immeasurable love of the Saviour, that radiates with a particular intensity from the immensity of his suffering, and through the mysteries of his risen life.

Pope John Paul II reminds us that "The Church never ceases to relive his death on the Cross and his Resurrection, which constitutes the content of the Church's daily life." *(Redemptor Hominis)* As for the Church, so for each of us; the goal of our living is that he becomes the content of our daily life; that he becomes the centre of our attention, the supreme object of our love. Mary, who shared his pain and his triumph, is the sure guide on our road to him.

The reflections in this book are a modest effort to explore the love of Jesus for us which shines through the dark shadows of his Passion, and to experience the paschal joy which, in his boundless love, he has won for us by his victory.

They may help to make us attentive to two invitations which he gave, first to his disciples, but which we may regard as addressed to each of us.

One invitation was to be with him in his darkest hour. "Behold, we are going up to Jerusalem; and the Son of man will be delivered to the chief priests and scribes, and they will condemn him to death" (Mt 20, 18). The other was to meet him in the joy and in the full Galilean sunlight of his risen days. "Behold, he is going before you into Galilee" (Mt 28, 7).

But, in the eternal Pasch, revelation will be complete. "Behold, he is coming in the clouds, and every eye will see him, every one who pierced him . . ." (Rev 1, 7).

Then even the brightest dawns that played on him as he stood by the lake of Galilee at Eastertide will pale before the splendid light of the eternal day. Then the pierced side will fully reveal the Heart that loves without limits, and will open our hearts to an unending response.

2 February, 1985   John Moloney

1 Furnished and Ready

So Jesus sent Peter and John, saying,
"Go and prepare the passover for us,
that we may eat it . . . and tell the
householder, "The Teacher says to you,
Where is the guest room, where I am to
eat the passover with my disciples?"
and he will show you a large upper room
furnished; there make ready.

Luke 22, 8, 11, 12

A feature of the central moments in the history of salvation is the idea of preparation. The divine preparation had a particular pattern. It was never hurried; there was careful attention to detail; it had the quality of reverence for the events that lay ahead. It was also God's loving way of helping man to understand the importance of the coming sacred event.

God sent Abraham on a journey. In three days of travel to the mountain of Moriah he had time, in

1

the silence of his heart, to dwell on the mystery of God's command. He was on a pilgrimage of faith, and every step of the road was an experience of faith that made his heart ready to sacrifice his son.

In the preparation of Mary for the divine motherhood God furnished her with every adornment.

For thirty years, in the silence of a hidden life, Jesus prepared for the moment when he would set out to preach the Good News. Before he started out on that mission he made himself ready by forty days of prayer and fasting.

Go and Prepare

When the supreme moment of his life was approaching he sent two of his disciples ahead to prepare for the Pasch. "So Jesus sent Peter and John, saying, 'Go and prepare the passover for us, that we may eat it'." They said to him, "Where will you have us prepare it?" He said to them, "Behold, when you have entered the city, a man carrying a jar of water will meet you; follow him into the house which he enters, and tell the householder, 'The Teacher says to you, where is the guest room, where I am to eat the passover with my disciples?' and he will show you a large upper room furnished; there make ready" (Luke 22, 8-12).

Peter and John, the great lovers, were chosen to prepare for the love feast. Short and clear as had been his invitation to come and follow him, so now were his words to go and prepare for the feast.

The care and precision of that instruction must have impressed on the apostles that an important event lay ahead. The external arrangements were but a sign of his own preparation for that moment. Often he had spoken of his hour, the hour towards which he looked forward with such an intense longing. His whole life, the whole direction of his prayer. had been a preparation for this hour. Now it had come.

With Desire

"And when the hour came, he sat at table, and the apostles with him. And he said to them, 'I have earnestly desired to eat this passover with you before I suffer'." (Lk 22, 14, 15). Having chosen them in love he fashioned them in love. They had a special place in his heart; he had made them his own, and so he loved them 'until the end'. He had captured their hearts, and they found themselves drawn irresistibly towards him. True, there were small vanities and ambitions to be overcome, and they were still short in courage which his gift of the Holy Spirit would later supply; but these rugged, simple men were deemed ready, worthy to share in his Priesthood, and to be the first recipients of his Body and Blood.

In that whole setting, what poverty! What humility! "Where shall we go?" The homeless Lord, with his homeless friends had to seek the hospitality of a poor man to celebrate the pasch. "Not a rich or powerful person was chosen," says St Ambrose, "but a poor man; and the small room of a poor man was preferred to the palace of the nobility."

Jesus sat down. It was truly a touching gesture of equality and friendship. He who had sat down on the ground at the well and made it easy for a sinful woman to come near him, now sat down with men whom, a few moments later, he would address not as servants but as friends. "With desire." Those words express the intensity of his joy, and contain, as well, a special revelation of the inexhaustible riches of his love. Like a river in flood, on that night there was no restraining the effusion of his love. So completely did it fill his soul that, for the moment, despite the nearness of his Sacred Passion, he put the thoughts of his sufferings into the background.

The room was ready. Now the final preparation for the supreme mystery of his love was to make ready the room of their hearts. They must be cleansed.

He Bent Down

He who was soon to humble himself on the Cross bent down to the level of their feet. That cleansing was a condition of their entering into partnership with him. Again we note the perfection of this divine ritual. St John gives a wealth of detail. Jesus 'rose from the supper, laid aside his garments and girded himself with a towel. Then he poured water into a basin, and began to wash the disciples' feet, and to wipe them with the towel with which he was girded" (Jn 13, 5). It was a dramatic gesture by which he prepared for the most sacred event of his life, and which, for all time, would be a reminder that he who came to pour clean water on a sinful world and offered himself as the spotless Lamb has the right to expect the preparation of cleansing by all who would approach the Table of the Eucharist.

St Augustine loved to dwell on every detail of that action; he saw it related to the whole saving mission of Jesus. "He laid aside his garments who when he was in the form of God, emptied himself; he girded himself with a towel, who took on the form of a servant. He poured out water into a basin to wash the feet of his disciples, who poured out on the ground his blood which washed the uncleanness of sinners. On the Cross he was stripped of his garments; in death he was wrapped in a winding-sheet; his whole Passion was our cleansing."

He washed his disciples' feet because they were worthy to be washed. They were about to be consecrated as ministers of the Table of the Eucharist; they were also to become bearers of the bread of the word. "How beautiful upon the mountains are the feet of him who brings good tidings" (Is 52, 7). Their feet would carry them across the hills to announce his Gospel to the world.

Message for All

The whole liturgy of preparation by which Jesus prepared his disciples for the institution of the Holy Eucharist has an application for us all. Every time we come to the celebration we have the blessed task of making ourselves ready. We have to prepare the upper room of our hearts which is to be furnished and ready for him when he comes. He should not have to arrive as an unexpected guest into a house in disarray. Each time we come we are responding to a divine invitation; there is the Lord's intense desire to eat the pasch with us. It is for us to ensure that his desire to come is matched by our desire to receive him.

A monk of the Eastern Church has given us some beautiful thoughts on the application of the gospel of the upper room to our lives. "It is not enough to prepare a corner of my soul, hiding away the disorder which exists in the other parts of myself. It is my whole soul that has to be washed clean . . . In some way or other, each soul has its secret rooms where dust and dirt accumulate, and which we would prefer not to open to anyone. There is danger in thinking of our communions as 'ceremonial visits,' when we are careful to receive Christ 'in the drawingroom,' in the front room. But, on the contrary, it is into the lowest places of our soul, into our 'chamber of horrors,' that we must allow Christ to enter.''

Another thought. When the Lord comes he is not alone. He comes ''with his disciples.'' So we have to open the doors of our hearts to a large company of guests, for the Eucharist is the celebration of the whole Church. The Lord, cleansing me, not only my feet, but heart and head, makes me worthy to share with him the task of washing the dust of the road off the feet of the world's pilgrims to the Holy Table. Through his exercise of sublime humility he makes us worthy of the sublime honour of having a part with him in washing the feet of men.

The more we reflect on the care and beauty of the divine preparation for the whole plan of salvation, and, in particular, on the exquisite care with which Jesus prepared his disciples for the institution of the Holy Eucharist, the more careful will be our approach to the Supper Room. Our reflection will create in us the urge for cleansing; we will not wish to come with feet unwashed, with soul unclean. It will stir up in us a sense of anticipation, a quickening of love, an intense desire to eat the Pasch with him. It will help to deepen in us a reverence which is the gateway to every expression of worship which the Mystery of Faith and Love deserves.

2 The Great Supper

Now before the feast of the Passover, when Jesus knew that his hour had come to depart out of this world to the Father, having loved his own who were in the world, he loved them to the end.

John 13, 1

There were two solemn nights on which history was made. One was the blessed night when God rescued his holy people from slavery and brought them safely across the path he had cut for them through the waters, and set them on their road to the land of promise. The other was the darkest night in the world's history, the night on which the Lord Jesus was betrayed. But against the background of that dark deed there shone forth the supreme mystery of the Lord's love. It was the splendid and blessed night of the Last Supper.

Jesus began by celebrating the mighty deed his Father had done for his people, the memorial re-enactment of the great deliverance, sealed in the blood of the lamb. Jesus, after he had eaten the Pasch with his disciples on that night did a much more mighty work. No longer through the blood of a lamb but through the power of his own blood he effected the passover of his people to his Father. In the moment of recalling a glorious past, a new world was beginning. The celebration of the Pasch was "but the shadow of the good things to come" (Heb 10, 1). Now the good things had come, and the tender memories of the Passover faded into shadows before the splendid light of the sublime revelation of divine love in the institution of the Holy Eucharist.

We might dwell with profit on every word and action of Jesus in that solemn moment.

"... *having loved his own.*" In choosing them he made them his own. They little realised how much more intimately they were to become his own; neither did they dream how intimately he was going to become their possession through this new mystery of his love. It was a moment of sacred exchange. These men had left all things to give themselves to him; now they were to receive their reward, nothing less than himself, whole and entire, under the appearance of bread and wine.

"... *until the end.*" That phrase takes one's vision of the Eucharist beyond time and space, opening up an ever-widening vista, from the Supper to the Cross and beyond, showing us how, through his death, we might have life, his very own life with which he loves and lives in his Father. Each one of us becomes his very own, until the end, till the very extremity of loving, until the end of our time, and of all time, until the final assembly for the Heavenly Supper. Then we shall have reached completion, and his word on the

Cross — "It is accomplished" — will have reached its consummation.

As Pope John Paul II puts it, "Rightly we believe that loving to the end means until death, until the last breath. The Last Supper teaches us, however, that for Jesus to the end means beyond the last breath, beyond death."

Here was the central event of his whole saving mission, and, as well, the deepest proof of his love. It was the pivotal moment of history towards which a world, waiting and prepared by many types, found fulfilment, and from which the christian life of all future generations would find meaning. A descriptive phrase of Pope John Paul II in his homily in the Phoenix Park, Dublin, sums up the marvel of that moment. "From the Supper Room in Jerusalem, from the Last Supper, in a certain sense, the Eucharist writes the history of human hearts and of human communities."

From the great supper went forth the great invitation, an invitation that transcended time and space. "Take, all of you, and eat." Wide as the embrace of his arms soon to be extended on the Cross was the extent of his desire to share himself with all until the end of time. Again Pope John Paul II illustrated the import of this mystery. "He loved his 'own' — those who were then with him — and all those who were to inherit the mystery from them. The words he pronounced over the bread and wine ... are precisely the revelation of this love through which, once and for all, for all time and until the end of the ages, he shared himself. Even before giving himself on the Cross, as the 'Lamb who takes away the sins of the world', he shared himself as food and drink; bread and wine, so that 'they may have life and have it abundantly' (Jn 10, 10). It was thus that he "loved to the end".

... Given to You

In that moment of sublime love Jesus offered himself in two directions, upwards and outwards. He presented himself as a sacrificial offering to his Father for the sins of the world; and he gave himself to his disciples and to us in the Sacrament of his Body and Blood.

For an understanding of the greatness of the Sacrament of the Holy Eucharist we have to keep in mind that the banquet table to which we are invited is also an altar of sacrifice. It is only from that altar that the Bread comes as the fruit of the Sacrifice. The same extreme of love that prompted our blessed Lord to offer his life on the Cross makes him give himself to us as the source of life. The inexhaustible stream of salvation from the side of the Saviour brings a superabundance of food for God's people. Inexhaustible love provides an unfailing supply of Divine Food. "They all ate and were satisfied" (Mk 6, 42). And because his love is indivisible he gives himself totally to each of us. 'He loved me and gave himself for me' (Gal 2, 20). Almost as if his Sacred Passion became my own possession and that there is no one to be saved but me alone. So he feeds me as if there were no other, sharing with me the totality of his own life. I come therefore to the Feast in answer to a personal invitation. In the divine democracy of the Eucharistic Banquet there are no reserved places at the table. There is the same welcome for the saint and the repentant sinner, the innocent child, the statesman and the theologian.

While he comes to each as a personal gift and enrichment it is true also that our taking and eating is a social act. We share in a family feast and we are deepening faith and love in the members of his Mystical Body, the Church.

House of Bread

Gently, as once at Bethlehem, which means house of bread, and with the same simplicity and humility, he came to this moment. The Supper Room became the new house of bread. At Bethlehem he came as Emmanuel, God with us; now he became God in us. Over bread and wine he spoke words which were at once an expression of love and a sign of power.

The Lord, aching with all the world's pain, parched with thirst for the love of human hearts, having completed his work, came forth victorious in all the strength and glory of Easter.

He meets the multitudes on all the world's hillsides, looking with compassion on all who are weary and faint; and he gives them the true satisfaction which comes only from the Living Bread. And they were satisfied. The Eucharist always brings the joy of sufficiency, while in that very moment, he draws us forward creating within us a new hunger. "Lord, give us this bread always" (Jn 6, 34).

Newness

Thus every time we receive the Holy Eucharist, the Last Supper becomes a new Banquet; a new world is ever opening out before us.

The Good Shepherd is always finding new pastures for his flock. On the mountains of the new Israel fresh and green are the pastures where he gives me repose.

St. Thomas Aquinas, in his hymn for the feast of Corpus Christi, describes under three headings the newness which the Eucharist brings: *"Let old things depart, let all be new, - hearts, words, works."*

The Lord makes the hearts of those who find him in the breaking of bread to burn with a new love, a new yearning to be united with him and to abide in his love. He puts on human lips a new song. He, who serves us with his own hands, gives a new impulse to our urge to reach out to serve the needs of human hearts.

Delight

In receiving him we taste and see that the Lord is sweet. The Manna was a sweet-tasting food; but it was only a shadow of the delight which the Bread of Life brings. He alone satisfies the deepest human hunger. The longing to possess him in the Sacrament corresponds to his intense desire to give himself; and the joy which was in his heart at the Last Supper, and at every Eucharistic Banquet, finds its echo in every heart which opens its doors to receive him. The disciples were glad when they saw the Lord; they were glad when they received the Lord. It was easy for them, as it is for us, to see how the Eucharist links the night of his suffering with the morning of his resurrection. He gives delight, he brings consolation to all who are heavy laden. Jesus, Bread that was broken, heals broken hearts.

3 Together in his heart

A new commandment I give to you, that you love one another; even as I have loved you, that you also love one another. By this all men will know that you are my disciples, if you have love for one another.

As the Father has loved me, so have I loved you; abide in my love.

John 13, 34, 35; 15, 9.

IN the very moment when God revealed his law he recalled the intimacy of his love for his people. When he promulgated his twofold command that man should love him with all his heart, and his neighbour as himself, he told Moses to remind the people "how I bore you on eagles' wings and brought you to myself. Now therefore if you will obey my voice and keep my covenant, you shall be my own possession among all peoples" (Ex 19, 4-5). Having borne his people in his arms with all the tenderness of a loving Father, and having made them a family all his very own, he had the right to expect them to reflect his love.

Right through the story of his care of them goes the idea that their care for and love of one another should mirror his love of them. Fraternal concern for the poor and outcast found its ideal in his unfailing care of them. "Love strangers because you also were strangers in the land of Egypt" (Dt 10, 18). That love was not simply a natural solidarity; its motive was sacred because it belonged to the history of salvation.

Drama of Love

In Jesus the drama of love was completed. On the night on which he gave the supreme proof of his love in the Sacrament of the Eucharist, it was fitting that he should make the supreme demand of love. He had never asked anyone to walk a road he himself had not travelled. Now in the setting of the supreme example of his love — the offering of his life — he was asking men to walk the road of love. He loves with a divine jealousy. The disciples whom he called he made to be his own, and now he bestows on them his own commandment. "This is my commandment, that you love one another as I have loved you" (Jn 15, 12).

They got a solemn mission to love each one whom he called his own. He had prepared them for this work of love, for he had given them a special revelation of his Father's love. "All that I have heard from my Father I have told you" (Jn 15, 15).

The fruitfulness of their whole apostolic mission would be related to their faithfulness to the ideal of fraternal love, and this, in turn, would make invincible the power of their intercession. "I...appointed you that you should go and bear fruit and that your fruit should abide; so that whatever you ask the Father in my name, he may give it to you. This I command you, to love one another" (Jn 15, 16, 17).

It was a command based on the highest ideal ever presented to human hearts, to love as Jesus loves; and to carry that love to the extreme limit of laying down life as he did for his friends. Here is the point where they meet the loving Christ in his noblest hour, and where they got the heroism to go to the extreme of laying down their own lives, thus giving to all of us an example of total fidelity to the Master's command. "By this we know love, that he laid down his life for us; and we ought to lay down our life for the brethren (1 Jn 3, 16).

New Commandment

"A new commandment I give you, that you love one another" (Jn 13, 34). Jesus opened up new vistas, never seen before, of the communion of love between the Father and Himself, and of the impulse of the Holy Spirit which drove him to lay down his life for his friends. The voice of the Father, telling how well pleased he was with his Son was new; the voice of the Son, telling how he always does what is pleasing to his Father, was also new. It was a new experience for mankind when the shedding of the Precious Blood of Jesus made every person precious and worthy to be loved. The wide spread of eagles' wings was matched by the arms of Jesus stretched wide on the Cross, gathering into one the whole family of the redeemed. This was the ultimate in giving which deserved the ultimate response in loving; here was the basis for all christian love till the end of time. Love of the brethren derives from, and returns to that communion of love which is the life of the Holy Trinity; and it puts the stamp of the Holy Trinity on the christian life. It brings it to perfection and brings also the reward of the fullness of joy.

René Voillaume presents this thought in very beautiful words: "As the Incarnate Word loves men, we, henceforth, are obliged to love them in our turn. We have here the point of departure of a command that is without limit. What is new is the fact that the image of God, imprinted upon man, is now complete, brought to perfection. Man has become, over again, in a true sense, the son of God."

Memories

St. John never forgot the love discourse of his Lord on the night of the Last Supper. He who had leaned on the breast of the Master, and had seen his side opened, retained vivid memories of the Lord's command, and in the clear vision of old age, he had only one message which he kept repeating. "Little children, let us love one another". "If God so loved us we also ought to love one another" (1 Jn 4, 11).

The new commandment presents the unity of source from which all christian love derives. "I have called you friends." In responding to his love we receive the gift of his abiding love and we discover in his Heart the motive for loving all his friends. We find our brothers in the Heart of Jesus,

and from him we receive the impulse to love them
without limit.

Cemented by Love

St. Augustine described the Church as a building
cemented by love. He likened christians to stones
newly quarried on the mountains or timber felled
in the forests. They are set in line and evened up by
workers. "But they do not make a house of God
unless they are cemented together by love. If those
beams of wood and stones of the Church were not
joined to one another in a definite pattern, if they
were not peacefully intertwined, if they did not, by
mutual attachment in a certain sense 'love' one
another no one would dare to put a foot inside. . .
Our Lord Jesus Christ, wishing to enter and dwell
in us, used to say as though by way of building, 'A
new commandment I give you, that you love one
another. You were there lying in ruins, decrepit, no
house for me. To be rescued from your state of ruin,
you must now love one another'."

Civilization of Love

The Church never loses her dream of leading men
towards a new world which alone can be realized
by obeying the new commandment. In our century
we have had the example of St. Pius X and Pope
Pius XII, across the havoc of two world wars,
trying to warm in love hearts frozen in hatred, and
striving to join men's hands in a handshake of
friendship. Pope Paul VI set before the world the
ideal of a civilization of love.

The Second Vatican Council with a keen

sensitivity for the needs of our world translated into clear language the demands of fraternal love related to the specific areas of human heartbreak which need an infusion of love. "Everyone must consider his every neighbour without exception as another self. . . . In our times a special obligation binds us to make ourselves the neighbour of absolutely every person, and of actively helping him when he comes across our path, whether he be an old person abandoned by all, a foreign labourer unjustly looked down upon, a refugee, a child born of an unlawful union, and wrongly suffering for a sin he did not commit, or a hungry person who disturbs our conscience by recalling the voice of the Lord: 'As long as you did it for one of these, the least of my brethren, you did it for me' " (Mt 25, 40).

Triangle of Love

Beside one another in the Crypt of St. Peter's Basilica are the tombs of Pope John XXIII, Pope Paul VI and Pope John Paul I. Their proximity was described as a triangle of love. How apt a title! Each of these great lovers gave an outstanding example of love for the Church and for the whole human family which so needs an infusion of love in these days.

The command to love one another first given to the apostles is addressed to each of us. An ideal not beyond us because his love has opened our hearts.

4 Revealing his love

*... The hour is coming when I shall no
longer speak to you in figures but tell
you plainly of the Father ... the Father
himself loves you, because you have
loved me and have believed that I came .
from the Father. I came from the Father
and have come into the world; again, I
am leaving the world and going to the
Father.*

John 16, 25, 27, 28

JESUS never ceased to explain the
purpose of his coming. His mission
was to draw aside the veil to show us his Father,
and by revealing the marvel of his Father's love for
him and for us, to draw us towards his Father's
loving embrace. In the unfolding of his own saving
mission he reveals his father as the source and
impulse of the extreme of love that made him lay
down his life to save us.

In one solemn moment he lifted up his eyes to
heaven and addressed his Father in a sublime

prayer of thanks. "I thank thee, Father, Lord of heaven and earth, that thou hast hidden these things from the wise and understanding and revealed them to babes. All things have been revealed to me by my Father; and no one knows the Son except the Father ... come to me all who labour and are heavy laden, and I will give you rest. Take my yoke upon you, and learn from me. ..." (Mt 11, 25-28).

The clean of heart and the poor in spirit deserved to see God. Those who possessed the candour and littleness of childhood would be rewarded with the wisdom of heart which would enable them to enter into the most profound mysteries that flashed forth like a meteor from those words of Jesus.

The Father is perfectly satisfied with his Son. He takes endless delight in knowing and loving him. No one knows the Son except the Father. The Son is always turned towards his Father in an infinite impulse of self-giving. This beloved Son was a perfectly sufficient object of his love, and of the exercise of his Fatherhood.

But out of sheer love the Father turned his gaze on us. such an effusion of love for us flowed from his heart that he sent his only Son, and thus the Father of mercies and God of all consolation revealed his Heart to his Son. For that reason he could invite all who are weary and heavy laden to come to him for refreshment. And, as well, he could give us the invitation to take his yoke upon us, that is, to share his Cross out of love, through which he would lead us to his Father.

Entrancing Vision

St John was so entranced by the vision of the union of Hearts of Father and Son, and the interchange of knowing and loving that coursed between them that he has preserved for us many discourses of Jesus which open to us that glorious vision. "The Father loves the son" (Jn 5, 20). "The Father loves me" (Jn 10, 17). There is no sounding the depths of the tenderness and glory of the Father's love lavished on his Son. That ineffable truth deserves a life-time of reflection.

The Son's gaze is ever towards his Father. He acts and loves like his Father. He does "only what he sees the Father doing; for whatever he does that the Son does likewise" (Jn 5, 20). The Father loves his Son, and he loves all those for whom he sent his Son. Having sent him to lay down his life for his sheep he associated himself with the saving work of Jesus. He loves him intensely for having gone forth and for laying down his life. "For this reason the Father loves me because I lay down my life" (Jn 10, 17). Here Jesus opens up a further vista of his Father's love.

Fatherhood

In the coming of the Son made man God not only entered human history but he gave it a divine heartbeat.

In one of his most tender and revealing parables Jesus expressed the role of fatherhood in the sublime example of merciful love. A son, leaving his father's home, wasting his substance, reduced to the condition of swine; and then, in a moment of repentance, returning with faltering steps towards his father's home. A tender image of a father, faithful to his fatherhood and faithful to his love, embracing a loved son and clothing him again.

Jesus himself had gone forth, in a sense, from home, from the bosom of the Holy Trinity, into a far country. The son in the parable went on the road of sin; but the divine Son took the road on behalf of sinners; and, as he returned clothed in blood-stained garments, he approached his Father, not with faltering steps and downcast eyes, but with intense joy, receiving the place of honour which he richly deserved. If the father of the prodigal son welcomed his wayward son with joy, with what intense love did the Eternal Father welcome his Son on his return home!

In his discourse after the Last Supper Jesus gathered together the threads of all his teaching on his Father. The moment of completion of God's loving design for our salvation had come, and, as Jesus prepared to embrace his Cross, his Father was glorified, and he glorified his Son. "Now is the Son of Man glorified, and in him God is glorified" (Jn 13, 31). He proved his love by a joyful and totally docile obedience. To obey is to love and to love is to obey. "I do as the Father has commanded me, so that the world may know that I love the Father" (Jn 14, 31). And then there was the breathtaking revelation. Not only does the Father love his Son, but he loves also all those who love his Son. "The Father himself loves you because you have loved me, and have believed that I came from the Father" (Jn 16, 27). Here was an expression of the solidarity of Jesus with his disciples. Jesus cannot be loved without their being loved also. Nothing short of the total outpouring of the Father's heart was to be theirs, which would reach to all those who would come after them whom the Father would recognize and reward as lovers of his Son. For all their shortcomings the disciples never lacked total faith and unquenchable love for Jesus, and now he rewarded those qualities by opening up before their eyes a most profound vision.

He had shown the road he had come; now as he was to depart on his return journey, he who is the Way, led them into all Truth, as the certain path of Life. He would be the model and assurance of fruitfulness of all prayer to his Father. Such love he has for his Son, so precious the Blood his Son shed for us; all we have to do is to go to him in his Son's name. "If you ask anything of the Father, he will give it to you in my name"(Jn 16, 23).

Paraclete

The completion of the revelation on that night was the promise of the Paraclete. The word describes an advocate who encourages us and pleads our cause. Jesus was the bridge-builder who made possible our access to his Father; he fulfilled the role of advocate; and as he was about to leave the world, he promised to plead with his Father to send another Paraclete. "And I will pray the Father, and he will give you another Paraclete" (Jn 15, 16).

And so the first and last pages of the story are linked. The Spirit descended in the form of a dove on Jesus as he began his mission. He descended as a gift on the Lamb of God. The Dove, always turned towards the Lamb, showed him to men. And now, in the solemn moment when he was to offer himself as the Immaculate Lamb, he promised that the Dove would descend again; the Holy Spirit would lead men into full knowledge of the great truths of salvation. "When the Spirit of truth comes, he will guide you into all truth" (Jn 16, 13).

The Spirit makes us aware of our new status as

the beloved children of the Father bought by the precious Blood of the Lamb; and he puts into our hearts a new word, "Abba, Father," by which we address our Father with an endearing salute which tells of our awareness of the intimacy of a Father's love.

Heart

What was revealed to the apostles on that blessed night was revealed to all of us; and we can never exhaust the beauty and importance of that dazzling moment. Simple words, but those condensed phrases of Jesus enshrined sublime truths that our world urgently needs to relearn.

We might sum up the solemn discourse of Jesus as a revelation of his Heart. He told us of the Father of mercies and God of all consolation. Because he shares everything with his Son, he gives his Son a Heart on fire with love of him and of us; and he ensures that the flame of love in our poor human hearts is kept alive by giving us the gift of the Spirit.

A writer of the Eastern Church puts it so very beautifully: "The Father's heart is the model which the heart of Jesus reproduces. Every beat of that heart is an impulse by which the Father gives himself. These heartbeats send forth to us the Son's Blood, vitalized by the breath of the Spirit."

5 Keep them safe

Holy Father, keep them in thy name, which thou hast given me, that they may be one, even as we are one.

I do not pray for these only, but also for those who believe in me through their word, that they may all be one...

Father, I desire that they also, whom thou hast given me, may be with me where I am...

John 17, 11, 20, 24

MOST of the prayer of Jesus was wrapped in a deep silence. He loved the silence of the hills, where, through whole nights, or in the dawning hours, he prayed alone; and there, unheard by human ears took place the dialogue between God and God.

On the night of the Last Supper he prayed; but on that night his voice was heard; it was made in the setting of the solemn liturgy of the institution of the Holy Eucharist. The night of the supreme revelation of his love was also the revelation of his prayer at its culminating moment. Following the deepest expression of his love in giving himself, there came from his Heart a sublime effusion of words in the presence of his disciples who listened in reverent silence. His anxiety that they would be kept safe prompted his solemn prayer to his Father. "He lifted up his eyes to heaven". (Jn 17, 1). With his gaze turned towards his loving Father he pleaded with him to keep them safe. The same strong, loving arms that would welcome and shelter them were soon to receive him as he left this world. "Father, into thy hands I commit my spirit". (Lk 23, 46).

Testament

The prayer of Jesus at the Last Supper was a kind of testament, a disposal of his property. The apostles had become his very own, and in that solemn moment before his death he wished to make provision for them. He had loved them until the end, and now that he was going from them he made sure that they would not be bereft of love. Nothing was too good for those men who had given themselves completely into his possession. Nothing less than the very love which his Father always bestows on him will be theirs also.

The Apostolic Prayer

In the prayer of Jesus at the Last Supper, often titled his "priestly prayer", or "apostolic prayer", his unbroken dialogue with his Father reached its highest point. It was a summary of his whole mission. As his life was directed towards the moment of his Passion, Death and Resurrection, so his prayer concentrated on assuring his Father of his will to offer himself in sacrifice, and in making an unending intercession for the salvation of mankind. Having revealed his Father, he now directed his solemn prayer to him. It welled up from the depth of his Heart, expressing his will to offer himself, which linked it with his prayer in the garden and on the Cross.

"Father, the hour has come" (Jn 17, 1). The prayer of past generations, all the sacrificial rites related to the expiation for sin and the restoration of holiness to God's people, now reached fulfilment.

Day of Atonement

A central feast in the liturgy of God's people had been the Day of Atonement, celebrated each year with a solemn feast which recalled to the consciousness of God's people their need of cleansing from sin, and brought a recovery of their status as a holy people. On that day the High Priest entered the holy of holies, and made a threefold atonement, "for himself, for his house, and for all the assembly of Israel" (Lev 16, 17). He carried the blood of a victim offered in sacrifice, and sprinkled the mercy seat; and to that ritual was attached the idea of the purification of the people. It was on that day that the High Priest was allowed to invoke the name of God.

Jesus brought all shadows to fulfilment. Now had come the perfect Day of Atonement, when the High Priest of the New Testament was to shed his own blood to purge the sins of men, and the pattern of his solemn prayer would also be threefold, for himself, for his apostles, and for his Church.

For Himself

Jesus prayed for himself. "Father, glorify thy Son so that thy Son may glorify thee" (Jn 17, 1). The Son had glorified his Father by revealing him perfectly through his life, and by turning men's eyes and hearts towards him. Having finished the work that his Father had given him to do he asked him to see him through this hour, the hour of his death, on to triumph in the glory of his Resurrection.

When Simon, the High Priest, came forth after having offered sacrifice, he was described as coming forth from the inner sanctuary "like the sun shining on the temple of the Most High" (Sirach 50, 7).

Still more resplendent would Jesus, glorified by his Father, come forth from the sanctuary of the tomb in the dawn of Easter Day.

For His Apostles

Then Jesus extended his prayer to his apostles. He presented them to his Father. He had glorified his Father by making his name known. They had come to know the Father through a deep commitment to him in faith and love. "I have manifested thy name to the men whom thou gavest to me out of the world ... and they have kept my word" (Jn 17, 6). They fully believed that Jesus came forth from his Father, with a special mission to be a Saviour. And so they now deserved to be the object of his prayer. They also needed his prayers. They are not presented to the Father as strangers; they belonged to him as fully as they belong to his Son, because in the divine ownership, all things are owned in common.

As he was placing in their keeping the vital triumph that would be the source of eternal life for the Church, he prayed his Father to keep them from harm. They would have to live in a hostile world, and carry the message in fragile vessels. Like the Master, who was allowed to endure rejection and the perversion of his message, so they should understand that they would have to face a like experience. By pleading with his Father to sanctify them in truth, Jesus made sure that they would not fail.

For the Church

In the third part of his prayer Jesus embraced the whole Church. From his open Heart there issued a universal prayer that included all those who would believe in him through all ages to come. In that moment the gaze of Jesus turned to each of us; the power of his intercession touched our lives, and therefore it deserves from us the same reverent attention as the apostles surely gave to his prayer for them. Our openness of heart to believe all those vital truths revealed by him on that night and which have reached us through the preaching of the apostles join us to him in a communion of faith and love. By our oneness of faith we are at once gathered into that intimate union of life that exists between Jesus and his Father, and at the same time become apostles of his message of salvation to the world. The programme of our christian life is to believe that he has been sent.

At the heart of St. John's gospel is the idea of the journeys of the Son of God. Jesus comes forth from his Father, and, having completed the work which his Father had given him to do, he returned. The prayer of Jesus is likewise built on those twofold journeys, related to our lives in him, which describe what we might call the programme and the reward.

He prayed his Father that we would be faithful to the programme of life which he presented; that we might become perfectly one with him and thus might proclaim to the world "that thou has sent me!" And for our fidelity to that programme, a reward beyond our wildest dreams, that nothing less than the love with which his Father loves him would be in us, ... "that the love with which thou hast loved me may be in them, and I in them" (Jn 17, 26).

The memory of that prayer, just as the memory of all that happened on that blessed night, should never leave us, for it recalls all that we need to know of what he did and said on our behalf.

Was there any more that he could have done? "For their sake I consecrate myself" (Jn 17, 19). He set himself apart and offered his life in sacrifice on the great day of Atonement on Calvary.

Was there any more he could have said? He prayed with an intense desire that we would all reach the home that he has prepared for us which will realize all our dreams. "Father I desire that they also, whom thou has given me, may be with me where I am ..." (Jn 17, 24).

Love never ends. The rainbow of his protecting intercession is ever in the skies. The unbounded love that inspired the prayer of Jesus on that night keeps him ever living to make intercession. He is always pleading for his Church that she would keep the truth safe for God's holy people, pleading for each of us that we would ever keep lifting our eyes to heaven, our hearts set on following his steps till we reach the presence of a Father who loves us with an everlasting love.

6 Gethsemane

*And when he came to the place he said
to them, "Pray that you may not enter
into temptation."*

*And he withdrew from them about a
stone's throw, and knelt down and
prayed, "Father, if thou art willing,
remove this cup from me; nevertheless
not my will but thine be done."*

*And there appeared to him an angel
from heaven, strengthening him. And
being in an agony he prayed more
earnestly.*

Luke 22, 40, 41 — 44

IN the setting of a garden the first sin
was committed. Conscious of their
guilt Adam and Eve "hid themselves from the
presence of the Lord God among the trees when
they heard him walking in the garden in the cool of
the day" (Gen 3, 8). Into another garden, the
garden of Gethsemane, went the Son of God in the
silence of the night, hiding himself in the trees, not
out of shame, but for a loving converse with his
Father, and where he would begin a great and

terrible combat to win back for man his lost paradise.

It was a night with two histories. When Judas left the Supper Room, "it was night," the dark night of betrayal, when men, whose hearts were frozen with hatred, completed their plot to destroy their Lord. When Jesus left the Supper Room it was a blessed night, the night that would usher in the dawn of his Resurrection.

During his agony his whole bearing showed a majestic calm. There was an inner peace in his union of will with his Father which characterised the whole pattern of his prayer.

The Great Drama

Gethsemane was like a drama with all the elements of great theatre.

As he went towards the Mount of Olives the joy of all that went before became clouded over. His distress at the coming dispersal of his apostles flowed into words, "You will all fall away because of me this night; for it is written, 'I will strike the shepherd, and the sheep of the flock will be scattered'" (Mt 26, 31). Once before he was described as being moved with compassion because the people were like sheep without a shepherd. Now the reality of that dispersal and abandonment by his own afflicted his heart, and was rendered all the more poignant by the bravado of Peter, "Even though they all fall away, I will not" (Mk 14, 29).

An additional cause of sorrow for the Lord was their inability to understand. Shortly before, he had addressed them as little children, and now, in truth, they are behaving as children do in the presence of great sorrow; they are unable to sense it and turn aside, or settle down to sleep.

The Chosen Three

As Jesus entered the garden he called Peter, James and John to come forward with him. They were allowed to be close to the dramatic revelation of the divine and human in him. He had prepared them well. They alone were with him at the bedside of the daughter of Jairus. They saw his divine power flash forth from him. "Child, arise" (Lk 8, 54). They saw the tenderness of his human Heart. He took her by the hand and told them to give her something to eat. On Tabor they saw his raiment become dazzling white so that they might not be scandalised to see his garments stained with blood as he lay prostrate in the garden. As they were descending from Tabor they saw nobody but "Jesus only," and now they were to see Jesus only, bereft of all the defences and splendour of his divinity, his heart, to its utmost depths, afflicted with anguish.

In that dread and solemn hour he was alone. He prayed alone, and his prayer was a meeting-place of his divine and human will. It expressed the reality of his humanity, and, at the same time, his total loving acceptance of his Father's will. He "began to be greatly distressed and troubled" (Mk 14, 33). In that moment he verified the striking words of St Paul, "He made himself sin." It was as if the terrible burden of the sin of the world was upon him.

There was the deep distress in his human heart caused by the impending failure and dispersal of his own apostles, the apostasy, the hardening of hearts closed against his whole message; and in the lonely abandonment of that moment he cried out to his Father, "My Father, if it be possible let this cup pass from me." The complete humanity of Jesus shone through this dark hour. The same Jesus who slept in the boat from sheer fatigue, whose heart was moved to tears at the grave of Lazarus, showed now the same sensitivity, the same capacity for sorrow at its deepest level.

Pope John Paul II has an interesting reflection on the prayer of Jesus to his Father, "It is possible to perceive here an expression of his indebtedness to his Mother, to whom he owed his humanity, together with that dread of suffering and death which is proper to human nature. He respected her right to the very end; in Gethsemane and on Mount Calvary. His suffering extended over the whole range of human sensitivity that had made him appreciative of little children, of the lilies of the field and of the birds of the air and of all the beauties of creation."

Jesus, fragile and vulnerable in his humanity, was unshakable in his will to accept the divine decree, "not what I will, but what thou wilt" (Mk 14, 36).

Three Approaches

Each of the three Evangelists who records the agony of Jesus adds his own detail, setting it within the general pattern of his own Gospel. Through each of them Jesus gives a particular insight into the tenderness of his love for his Father, and his concern for all of his disciples, shown in that moment when he was flattened in anguish.

For Mark the agony of Jesus was intensified by the dispersal of his flock, and by their inability or unwillingness to understand the inner meaning of his mission. That unwillingness was exemplified in their falling asleep at the crucial test of his life. And then the final detail, that particular experience of sorrow felt in the failure of friends. "And they all forsook him, and fled."

Father David Stanley, S.J., in his book *Jesus in Gethsemane,* gives a masterly analysis of the inner meaning of the returns of Jesus to his sleeping disciples. "Mark presents Jesus as the Good Shepherd who, confronted with the divine threat of the destruction of his flock, returns repeatedly to look after it, to see if they are still together and safe. Jesus is the loving Shepherd filled with pity and concern for his own."

Mark alone tells us of the term of endearment, "Abba", used by Jesus to address his Father. It expressed the familiarity and companionship which gave him solace in that hour. As for the disciples, he did not need their companionship. What he wished for them was that they would understand their need of companionship with him through the power of his prayer, and through their learning the lesson he was teaching them of their vital need for unfailing perseverance in prayer.

Matthew relates how Jesus twice addresses his Father as "My Father." Again, as Fr. Stanley points out, "Matthew puts more emphasis on Jesus leaving his disciples for prayer to be with his Father. The Matthean Gethsemane is a kind of catechesis on the place of prayer in the Christian life . . . the Christian being schooled by the example of Jesus to experience in his prayer his adoptive sonship."

St. Luke's picture of Jesus at Gethsemane completes his picture of Jesus at prayer which is the special quality of his Gospel. He set out to present Jesus teaching prayer by praying;

36

instructing on prayer by his example. The hours of prayer before dawn, and the whole nights spent in prayer were gathered into the short phrase 'as was his custom,' with which he introduces his narrative. As his agony reached a sweat of blood his prayer reached its deepest intensity. "Being in an agony he prayed more earnestly."

Watching with Him

In the agony and prayer of Jesus in the garden we were all present. It is for us to return again and again. To all of us he keeps addressing his pleading, "Could you not watch?"

No dark hour of our sorrow that he had not known on that night; no fatigue in our prayer that the example of his praying the longer cannot dispel.

7 The Traitor's Kiss

Then Jesus, knowing all that was to befall him, came forward and said to them, "Whom do you seek?" They answered him, "Jesus of Nazareth."

Jesus said to them, "I am he." Judas, who betrayed him, was standing with him. When he said to them, "I am he," they drew back and fell to the ground. Again he asked them, "Whom do you seek?" and they said, "Jesus of Nazareth."

So the band of soldiers and their captain and the officers of the Jews seized Jesus and bound him.

John 18, 4-7, 12

WHOM do you seek? Three times in the Gospel Jesus addressed those words to those who sought him. The settings in which they were spoken were very different as were also the responses which they evoked.

Twice they echoed in the hearts of lovers. In the quiet of evening they were addressed to Andrew and his brother as they walked along the bank of the Jordan. A divine question that aroused the curiosity of his first lovers, followed by a divine invitation that led them to the heart of their Saviour.

In the garden on Easter morning Mary Magdalen, mourning and weeping and searching, came face to face with her risen Lord. And again, the same question, "Whom do you seek?" (Jn 20, 15). On this occasion also they led on to a revelation of his identity. One word more was enough. Jesus said to her, 'Mary'; she recognized him and her heart overflowed with joy.

But the third time Jesus asked the question was in the darkness of the blackest night in the world's history, and his words were addressed, not to lovers, but to men with murder in their hearts.

The arrest of Jesus is a subject almost too terrible to dwell upon. It was the ultimate contradiction of truth. Man, fashioned in love, who had been given the gift of freedom, had forfeited that freedom when he became enslaved by sin. Jesus, out of sheer love, came to free all prisoners and bring deliverance to captives, and in the very moment when he went forth to effect the great deliverance, man would lay hold of him and lead him forth to death.

It was a terrible moment when violent men laid hands on the hands of their Lord, and bound him and led him away.

The Key

But however much we would wish to turn away from the scene of the arrest of Jesus we must dwell on it, for it contains the key to our understanding of his sacred Passion and Death. While Jesus stood ready to become a victim of the power and cruelty of men he showed himself at the higher level at which he exercised total dominion over events. There was about the whole bearing of Jesus a sovereign calm as he showed a serene control over the horrible sequence of events that now began, and over the persons who were at the centre of the drama. At every step, Jesus, Lord of history, and master of the history of that night displayed a divine initiative, and in every detail of the events that followed he showed himself the master.

I am He

It was Jesus who spoke first. "Whom do you seek?" and to their reply, "Jesus of Nazareth", he said to them "I am he." And through the darkness of that night and on the darkness of their hearts there flashed forth from those words of Jesus an indication of his divinity. And before the majestic power of the Lord they fell back in dismay. "They drew back and fell to the ground." Lovers of Jesus often expressed gratitude or adoration by rushing forward and falling at his feet. But the enemies of Jesus fell backwards suddenly like a routed army in disarray.

St Augustine has given us a magnificent analysis of the inner meaning of the arrest of Jesus. "Where now are the cohorts of soldiers and guards of the Priests and Pharisees? Where is the terror that was meant to be inspired by this display of force? One voice that said 'I am he' was enough to repel and fell to the ground that crowd possessed by hatred and carrying terrible weapons. God was concealed in flesh, and the eternal day was so clouded from those human eyes that the powers of darkness, in order to kill him, had to search for him with lanterns and torches."

Jesus, standing unperturbed before a crowd who had murder in their hearts, was not merely displaying the steeling of nerves, the iron courage of a human hero in the presence of danger. His words 'I am he' expressed a manifestation of his divinity and was the source of his inner calm, and his dominion over the events as they are unfolded by St John. The very men who came to seize him were, without realising it, in his hands.

Twice Jesus repeated his questions, "Whom do you seek?" Eyes that were blind were not helped by lanterns to recognise their Lord; ears that had been closed against his message did not recognize his voice. It required the eyes of Judas to identify him for them. And he gave them the sign that has gone down in history, the betrayer's kiss. The sacred sign of love became a kind of sacrilege. Through a kiss, which should be the instrument of peace, the first violent touch, the first wound, was inflicted on the Lord.

Two Details

Two more details complete the picture, depicting his control over the events of that scene, as well as conveying two touching expressions of his compassion. It was not the crowd who gave instructions to a captive; it was Jesus who calmly issued orders to them. "If you seek me, let these men go."

This was to fulfil the word which he had spoken, 'Of those whom thou gavest me I lost not one'. In that dark moment he was able to turn with delicate compassion towards his own. Loving them until the end, he was making sure that they would be safe at the end.

When Peter struck off the ear of the servant of the High Priest, the same calm voice of the Lord told him "Put your sword into its sheath." Just as he was about to submit to being seized he affirmed his total freedom to complete his mission. "Shall I not drink the cup which the Father has given me?"

And then the final gesture of compassion; the last time that virtue went out from the touch of his hand before his hands were bound, the healing that preceded the healing of us all. "And he touched his ear and healed him" (Lk 22, 51).

The final details were told in two brief phrases almost as if the Evangelist wished to hurry past the horror of the arrest of Jesus. "They seized him and led him away." It was a terrifying summary of how evil poisons the hearts of men and of how love prompted our blessed Lord to abandon himself to his Father's will, the same love that made him abandon himself now into the hands of men.

The second phrase was equally brief. "Then all his disciples forsook him and fled" (Mt 26, 50). Forsaken in the garden; forsaken on the Cross.

Just as every episode in the sacred Passion reveals to us the tenderness of his love, so also does his arrest. Because our Faith is alive we need no lanterns or torches to discover him, and we cannot come close to him in that moment without being enriched with a new vision of his patience, of his serene calm, of the sensitivity of his love shown alike to enemies who bore in upon him and to friends who fled from him. His general invitation to us to bear the Cross with him includes an invitation to share with him something of the sorrow and isolation he endured in the moment of his arrest.

Our Darkest Hours

There can come dark moments in our lives when we feel that the powers of darkness close in upon us, and we are deserted even by our friends, and we stand defenceless and alone. Then his words "I am he," sound in our ears, but their effect is to draw us close to him for support. They reveal to us the inspiration of his example that will help us also to be in serene control of events, and also the comforting truth that the merits of his sacred Passion are at work within us ensuring our triumph in our darkest hours.

8   Truth on trial

Pilate said to him, "So you are a King?"
Jesus answered, "You say that I am a
king. For this I was born, and for this I
have come into the world, to bear
witness to the truth. Every one who is of
the truth hears my voice."
Pilate said to him, "What is truth?"

John 18, 37, 38

WITH a touch of his hand Jesus
opened eyes that were blind, and
those who looked on him for the first time loved
and praised him and followed after him. But not
even the touch of his most tender compassion
could heal the inner blindness of heart of those
who, from the very beginning of his earthly life,
closed their eyes and their hearts against him and
against his mission of universal healing from sin.
A mixture of pride and envy built up into an
implacable hatred in the Pharisees and chief
priests, who should have been leading the people
towards the Light Who had come into the world,

but instead, became blind guides luring people into the darkness.

Their first sin was to become enemies of the truth; so he who came to give testimony to the truth was assailed by the enemies of the truth. From the moment that he opened his mouth to teach, the inner truth in regard to himself and his message was put on trial. They struck at the truth of his divinity. "The Jews sought all the more to kill him, because he . . . called God his Father, making himself equal with God" (Jn 5, 18). In the very exercise of his mercy they tried to pervert his purpose. When he cured a withered hand they attacked him for healing on the Sabbath. That occasion was the one time the Gospels refer to anger in him. "And he looked around at them with anger, grieved at their hardness of heart" (Mk 3, 5).

God on Trial

The beginning of all sin was to put God on trial, to challenge the truth of his loving design. The tempter slipped into the heart of Eve the thought that God could be lying. "God knows that when you eat of it your eyes will be opened and you will be like God" (Gen 3, 5). The final moment of the combat that overcame sin was when the Son of God was put on trial, and with him the truth of his redeeming love went on trial.

A terrible moment in history was when Jesus was led away to trial. Then began a drama in four acts, as he was paraded, in quick succession, before four judges, each indulging his own particular travesty of justice. A drama of violent contrasts; the offering of the just for the unjust; the crescendo of cries for his death, and in the midst of that chorus of hatred, the serene silences of the Accused; and in the moments of terrible suffering and vile mockery, his regal calm and dignity.

The Judges

From Annas to Caiphas to Pilate to Herod, each with his special refinement of cruelty and the venom of sacrilegious words. Lie piled on lie, blow upon blow; but in the midst of frenzied cries and the thirst for blood he stood in regal majesty, preaching his final message, sometimes by silence, sometimes by words, words written in blood in human hearts, an everlasting testament to truth and love.

Before Annas Jesus received the first blow ever dealt him by human hands. "One of the officers standing by struck Jesus with his hand" (Jn 18, 26). Human hands can do ignoble deeds.

On to Caiphas. The High Priest and the elders, meticulous about legal observances, had no qualms about searching for false witnesses against Jesus. But even those who swore against him contradicted one another. But at last two came forward and said, "This fellow said, I am able to destroy this temple of God and to build it in three days" (Mt 26, 61). From Caiphas a question "I adjure you by the living God, tell us if you are the Christ the Son of God?" When Jesus confirmed who he was, the God who would one day be seen, not in this degraded condition, but in the clouds of heaven, the light of his risen glory filtered through the darkness of that moment.

Peter's Tears

While the shrieks of blasphemy were being hurled at him there came the voice that must have caused him even deeper grief — the voice of Peter denying his Lord. The denial of Peter is an exquisite miniature of divine mercy and human repentance While his Lord stood accused, Peter was on trial; the truth of his allegiance to his Lord was put on trial, and in a rush of words Peter sought the way of denial; the swift recourse to a lie that led him on to a curse. And, in contrast, another of the silences of Jesus. "And the Lord turned and looked at Peter" (Lk 22, 62). It was enough. Wordless sorrow and repentance. Love has eyes; sorrow has tears. Peter "went out and wept bitterly" (Mt 26, 75). And so, perhaps, the comfort of the first tears in the passion story may have eased the pain of the first blow he had received.

From Caiphas to Pilate. With the power of decision of life and death in his hands Pilate stands before history, a combination of weakness, contempt, evasion, ambition, affirming innocence and invoking sentence. Truth went on trial on that day when he who is the Truth was convicted for giving testimony to the truth.

"Take him yourselves and judge him" was Pilate's first effort at evasion, but they astutely threw the onus back on him. "What accusation do you bring against this man?" And the sworn enemies suddenly became the promoters of allegiance to Caesar. To the question asked in contempt, "Are you the king of the Jews?" Jesus opened up a glorious vision of the inner truth of his kingdom. "My kingdom is not of this world . . . for this I was born . . . to bear witness to the truth" (Jn 18, 36, 37). He needed to say no more. In the face of further accusations Jesus was silent. When Pilate admitted, "I find no cause in him," he was relentlessly pursued by the chief priests. "He stirs up the people, teaching throughout all Judea, from Galilee . . ." (Lk 23, 5).

Pilate seized on the mention of Galilee as another way of escape. When he heard that he was in Herod's jurisdiction he sent him away to Herod. A new indignity. Herod hoped to see a sign. His only interest was in a spectacle, a new curiosity to amuse him, a frivolous pastime to pander to his sensuous vanity. The majestic silence of Jesus was too much for him. The prisoner must be led back to Pilate.

Pilate offered them Barabbas, but they would have him release a criminal while they would do their God to death. And then, one final ruse, the ultimate trial of truth. "I will chastise him and release him" (Lk 23, 22). The Evangelists, as if wishing to hurry past the horror, describe the scourging of Jesus in one sentence. "Then Pilate took Jesus and scourged him" (Jn 19, 1).

Behold

When the Roman soldiery had done their brutal worst, Pilate presented him to the crowd, thinking that his piteous condition would move them to pity. But man, at that moment, had no pity on God. He who had compassion on the multitude received no compassion from this multitude.

"Behold the man," was an invitation addressed, not only to those clamouring for his death, but to all future generations who would look on him and love him. "Behold your king!" There would come countless generations who would see the crown of thorns as a diadem of love, and would adore this King whom they would recognise as never more resplendent than in this moment of dishonour.

Pope John Paul II has aptly described the deep

truth that lay beneath this mockery of truth: "Here we have before us the Christ in the truth of his kingship. . . . All the kingliness of men, all man's dignity — which Jesus came to express and renew — are here summed up in him. The price paid for dignity is the blood of the Son of God!"

"His blood be upon us" was the terrible imprecation of the accusers of Jesus. It is the noble prayer of the lovers of Jesus. And it is always answered, because the Blood comes from the Heart which is an inexhaustible source.

9 Road of Pain

*So they took Jesus, and he went out,
bearing his own cross, to the place
called the place of a skull, which is
called in Hebrew Golgotha. There they
crucified him, and with him two others,
one on either side, and Jesus between
them.*

John 19, 17, 18.

A phrase, very short, very striking,
describes the beginning of the road
to Calvary. "Jesus went out bearing his own
cross." Simple words that say so much. Behind
them lies a whole world of the revelation of that
final impulse of the heart of Jesus as he took the
road to Calvary.

The phrase conveys the sense of eagerness, of
the enthusiasm and inner joy that was in his Heart
as he laid hold of the Cross. It was not thrown on
unwilling shoulders. The tree that had made man
an enemy in Eden became the friend of the

Redeemer. The wood of the Cross was for him the precious instrument through which he would take sin away. For Jesus the cross was the "dulce lignum," the 'sweet wood' which the Church would sing of in her Good Friday Liturgy.

As Jesus set out for Calvary, the quest for the lost sheep was ending, and the Good Shepherd was on his way home rejoicing. As St Gregory Nazianzen reminds us, "When the good shepherd found the stray sheep he carried it on those same shoulders that bore the wood of the Cross." And in that moment of pain as he travelled the 'via dolorosa' there was in his Heart the joy of the shepherd over the return of so many lost sheep, and with him in that rejoicing the whole of heaven joined.

All the journeys of God's people converged on that road. All the longings for the land of promise would be fulfilled when Jesus on Calvary would open up the glorious vision of the new land of promise. The road which Isaac had travelled to the mountain of Moriah now merged with the road to to the mountain of the Lord.

The beloved son of Abraham carried the wood for the sacrifice; now the beloved Son of God carried the wood on which he would himself be offered as victim.

Three Mountains

Pope John Paul II speaks of 'the liturgy of three mountains' — Moriah, Tabor and Golgotha, which recalls three solemn and central moments in the history of salvation. At Moriah the father was well pleased with his prophet's obedience. "Now I know that you fear God, seeing that you have not withheld your son, your only son, from me" (Gen 22, 12). At Tabor the Father expressed his pleasure in his son, making the splendour of his glory to throw its beams forward beyond the darkness of Calvary, and thus gave to Tabor a Paschal character.

Like the journey to Moriah and the ascent of Tabor was the journey of Jesus to Calvary, which was the meeting-place of death and victory, of sacrifice and glory. He went forth, travelling a lonely road, wending his way through the pathways of men, he who had so often been surrounded by multitudes as on the hillsides, longing for his words and hungering for bread; now they were hungering for his blood.

Divine and Human

As Jesus carries his cross we are aware of the interplay of the human and divine in him. There is the human weakness, his body racked with pain, drained of strength, the fairest of the sons of men now disfigured almost beyond recognition. There is the divine resolve. Like a climber who summons a new impulse as he sees the summit just ahead, so does Jesus make the final ascent. How do we describe this final journey of Jesus? It is the road of pain and debasement and abject humiliation, the refinement of cruelty that reveals the heart of man who has no mercy on God. And yet it is a royal road, for the King is on his victorious journey home.

"Who is this that comes from Edom in crimsoned garments from Bozrah, he that is glorious in his apparel marching in the greatness of his strength? Why is thy apparel red, and thy garments like his that treads in the wine-press?" (Is 63, 1, 2). His garments are crimsoned in his own blood and therefore he is glorious in his apparel, and he marches, sustained by the divine strength to finish the work which his Father had given him to do. "Why is thy apparel red?" The vine harvester's garments become crimsoned as he treads in the wine-press. The Divine harvester is crimsoned by his own blood as he treads the wine-press alone, and in that glorious moment in the harvest of the Cross gives the new wine that will delight his people for all time, and will never run short.

Two Moments

Two moments on the road to Calvary, described by the Gospels, relieve the horror and the hatred that had poisoned so many human hearts. The divine condescension of Jesus had so often been shown in his willingness to accept human partners, and so we find him now accepting the partnership of a pair of hands, and the compassion expressed in women's tears.

Simon of Cyrene, chosen from the motley crowd, was the first to share the burden of the cross of Jesus. His name has gone down on record, but, more than that, the prints of his hands are written into the wood.

Like a ray of sunlight in a dark sky is the story of the tears of the women of Jerusalem. "And there followed him a great multitude of the people, and of women who bewailed and lamented him" (Lk 23, 27). When there was no voice to speak for him they spoke through their tears an eloquent and consoling message. Their lament represented that tenderness, the special quality of women, which at that moment, as in every moment of history, expressed a refinement, a compassion, when men's hearts are turned to stone and they can do foul deeds. The tears of mothers had lamented the slaughter of their children at the moment of his coming; they took up the lament of Rachel mourning for her children because they were not; and now there was the lament of women again, this time for the Innocent One who was being led to the slaughter. The women of Jerusalem take their place in a special Roll of Honour with the women of Galilee who had served him and, like the three Marys at the Cross, they stayed with him until the end — the service of presence combining with the service of compassion.

St Luke who had shown Jesus bestowing compassion on the apostles in Gethsemane, now again shows him bestowing rather than seeking compassion. "Daughters of Jerusalem, do not weep for me, but for yourselves and for your children" (Lk 23, 28).

We can return with profit to those two stopping-places of Jesus on the road to Calvary. To each of us, at some moment, is given the blessed privilege of Simon; to be allowed, through pain, or the burden of sorrow, to share the Cross of Jesus, we can become a Simon by lending a hand to someone who is weary and heavy laden. And we can be sure that by virtue of the Cross he bore, Jesus makes our burdens, all burdens, light. It is certain that he who rewarded the centurion's act of faith also rewarded Simon's act of service. Our act of service of the cross springs from an inner vision of faith that shows us the value of entering into the mystery of that suffering by which he saved the world.

We give him support; we also receive. When we realize that the tip of the beam of our cross rests on the shoulders of Jesus, we are never crushed. For the gift of our hands he gives us strength to finish our road to Calvary. For the gift of compassion he gives to our eyes a fountain of tears that flows back on ourselves to bedew our repentant hearts.

Crowded Road

The road to Calvary is ever thronged, for, like it or not, it is the road that everyone who longs for peace and cleansing and the sharing in the new life of the risen Lord must travel. And for lovers of the Lord it is a daily journey, a constant companionship; for there is an urge in us to want to be close to a dear one in a moment of trial or pain; to lend a hand, if possible to relieve his suffering; to give him the comfort of compassionate love.

10 Today in Paradise

One of the criminals railed at him, saying "Are you not the Christ, save yourself and us!"

But the other rebuked him, saying "... we are receiving the due reward of our deeds; but this man has done nothing wrong."

And he said, "Jesus, remember me when you come in your kingly power."

And he said to him, "Truly, I say to you, today you will be with me in Paradise."

Luke 23, 39-43

WHEN Jesus was raised on the Cross his arms were extended; they enfolded the whole human family in a universal embrace. They represented mercy extending as far as east is from the west. Stretching out before his eyes was the panoramic vision of a multitude that no man could number; the loving glance of his merciful love in that moment, reaching from generation to generation into the past; and taking in the countless generations to come.

And yet in that very moment of universal redemption he turned his gaze towards one person, a poor criminal, dying beside him. Marvellous but not strange, for his Father had always revealed himself as a God who has an individual, personal care of the least as well as of the greatest. While directing the movements of the mighty planets he has a care also for the humble wayside flowers.

Knowing by Name

A moving psalm which describes his knowledge of the stars describes him as bending down to comfort the brokenhearted. "He heals the broken-hearted and binds their wounds. He determines the number of stars, he gives to all of them their names" (Ps 147, 3, 4). The God who knows the stars by name is so great and yet so tender that he has a care for one broken heart, one open wound. Nothing can stop the forward surge of his love as he comes close to the individual. "I will go before you and level the mountains, I will break in pieces the doors of bronze and cut asunder the bars of iron. . . . I call you by your name, I surname you. . . ." (Is 45, 2, 4).

The same theme of individual caring follows like a golden thread through the public ministry of Jesus. The Good Shepherd of the flock had a care for, and time for, the one sheep. No matter how engaged he was in preaching to the multitude, he instantly responded to a plea to go to heal one sick child. And now the Good Shepherd who had promised to seek out one lost sheep turned towards a lost sheep dying beside him. He turned the whole power of his redeeming love on just one abandoned criminal.

The Great Dialogue

The public life of Jesus had begun with a dialogue, "Rabbi, where are you staying?" (Jn 1, 38) and now in the closing moments of his life there took place a dialogue equally decisive, a perfect drama enacted with few words.

While one of the criminals joined with the crowd in the chorus of blasphemy and mockery "the other rebuked him, saying, 'Do you not fear God since you are under the same sentence of condemnation? And we indeed justly; for we are receiving the due reward of our deeds; but this man has done nothing wrong'." Before he asked for pardon he already professed his faith. A poor criminal, justly condemned became the just judge of the innocence of his Lord, a glorious witness to the truth. How his words must have comforted him who had endured in silence the false witnesses who had been used to bring about his condemnation. The good thief did not cry to him to come down from the cross; the inner vision of faith put different words into his mouth. Through the darkening shadows Jesus became visible in his mercy, and so he opened his dialogue with his Saviour in a simple plea that came straight from his heart. "Jesus, remember me when you come in your kingly power."

He did not ask to be forgiven but only to be remembered, and thus, this voice, quivering in pain, entered into the great song of praise of the Lord in his remembering. Jesus had become visible to him in the full truth of his saving mission. The Good Shepherd, as he was giving his life for his sheep, looked on the lost sheep with compassion and was recognized by him. The lost sheep recognized the shepherd and professed his deep faith in his saving power. St John Chrysostom beautifully describes his plea. "You look on the crucified but profess your Lord. You see the figure of the condemned and you profess the divinity of the King." The response to his pleading came quickly. "Truly I say to you, today you will be with me in Paradise." Truly the Lord comforted the broken-hearted. Across the span of centuries two comments on the marvel of that moment. St Ambrose said: "Quickly the Lord forgave because the thief was quickly converted. The Lord always gives more than he is asked for. To be with Christ is life; and where Christ is, there is his kingdom." A great French orator said: "Today! What promptitude! With me! What company! In Paradise! What repose!"

Two Freedoms

A dying man whose hands were fastened used to full advantage the only freedom that remained to him, the freedom of heart and tongue. "Man believes with his heart and so is justified, and he confesses with his lips and so is saved" (Rom 10, 10). This man believed with all the intensity of a truly repentant heart, and for the humble confession he professed with his lips he received salvation. He was the last human being to address a word to the dying Saviour, and his words take their place for all time in the honoured company of the seven last words of Jesus on the Cross.

They were heard and recorded by John, who had already enjoyed Paradise on earth by being "with Jesus," his heart totally given. They were heard by Magdalen who knew what it was to be remembered and forgiven. And surely they were heard by Mary; and, for her, what consolation to hear, amid the blasphemies all around her, just one voice proclaiming that "this man has done nothing wrong," to hear words that opened up a vision of his kingly power, and brought her in that moment of anguish, the joy of seeing the first of her newfound sons safely home. "Behold your son." Her maternal love and embrace were given not only to John, the apostle of pure love, who took her to his own home, but also to the repentant thief, the witness of pure repentance, whom her Son took to his own home before the sun went down on that day of salvation.

But they have been treasured also by all succeeding ages; they have become a dialogue of salvation that has given courage and strength to every sinner who has stood before the Cross in need of being remembered, and no longer afraid to ask for pardon.

The whole episode might be seen as having the elements of sacramental Confession. There is the preparation of faith, hope, charity. The good thief was led by faith to believe that he who was dying beside him was the Lord to whom belonged the kingdom; through hope he longed for and obtained a place in that kingdom. He exercised charity towards his fellow criminal, trying to lead him to conversion. After such preparation he was ready to confess his guilt. He acknowledged the cross as a just reward for his sins.

And then he could present himself with heartfelt petition for pardon. Such a humble and contrite heart was not despised by the Lord; it received instant absolution and the certainty of a glorious reward. The apostles whom he had chosen out of love he made to be "with him". The poor criminal whom he chose to be the apostle of his pardon he promised would be "with me" and that meant, not merely sharing a companionship with him, but sharing his own very life.

Was there ever such an individual confession, such a personal encounter, so close to the Heart of the Saviour in the moment when his Heart was opened to cleanse all hearts with the floodtide of his pardon?

The history of the penitent thief is the experience we all have, time and again, in the Sacrament of Penance. It is for all of us; in the words of Pope John Paul II, "our personal encounter with the crucified, forgiving Jesus." One repentant thief beside him, one Magdalen at the foot of the Cross, was worthy to receive the total riches of his forgiving love. So also am I.

11 Throne for a King

*After this Jesus, knowing that all was
now finished, said (to fulfil the
scripture), "I thirst." A bowl full of
vinegar stood there; so they put a
sponge full of the vinegar on hyssop and
held it to his mouth.*

*When Jesus had received the vinegar,
he said, "It is finished"; and he bowed
his head and gave up his spirit.*

John 19, 28-30.

'**A**nd I, when I am lifted up from
earth will draw all men to
myself' (Jn 12, 32). Jesus promised to draw us.
From the moment he was raised on the Cross that
movement began; and everyone who has
responded to the magnetism of that impulse has
begun by looking on him with love, and directing
attention to the words and actions that were part
of his final moments on the Cross. These actions
have a profound meaning; his words are like an
inexhaustible fountain that contains new depths
for those who would dwell on them.

Only a few days previously he was teaching
daily in the Temple, and never was his preaching
more eloquent than in those brief words spoken
from the Cross. So often he had ascended a
mountain to teach the multitudes; never was his

preaching so related to his saving mission than when he ascended Mount Calvary.

His precious seven words were not drowned in the clamour of mockery and curses that filled the air; for there were some hearts in whose silent depths his words sounded and were stored.

Having turned his loving gaze on one repentant thief, he then looked towards his Mother, arranging to provide a home for her, and a home for all the redeemed in his Mother's arms. And in that very moment in which he provided the companionship of Mary for the Church he expressed the final depths of abandonment.

Well and Temple

Twice before he had spoken of thirst. At Jacob's well he had asked a woman for a drink. The well and the Cross have many features in common. Jesus, at the sixth hour, was tired from the journey. His never-ending quest for the souls of men had taken him through dusty sun-baked roads, unending roads, crowded with fugitives fleeing from the gentle persuasion of his love. The eternal pattern of love's journey never changes, always the Divine Lover seeking him whom his soul loves.

To relieve his fatigue Jesus sat down, and in that very gesture he, who reigns among the Cherubim, was content to sit on the ground as his throne. It was the humility of him who would soon humble himself even unto the death of the Cross. Seated on the ground he was accessible at the level of human life. And it was there he was found by the woman of Samaria.

"Jesus said to her, 'Give me a drink.' " (Jn 4, 7).

"He who asked her for a drink thirsted for her faith," said St Augustine. The thirst of the Saviour brought the conversion of a sinner, and created in her heart a thirst for the truth.

It was all so like what would happen at Calvary. There, at the sixth hour, the fatigue of his final journey was upon him. He lay down on the Cross as his supreme act of abasement. He did not need nor drink the water from the well; neither did he require the drink offered him on the Cross. His deepest thirst was to be thirsted for. The episode at the well closed with a solemn profession of faith by a woman with a new-found faith. She, through the grace of that encounter with Jesus, travelled a long journey, from a lack of understanding to a beginning of understanding, and a deep hope for vision. "I know that Messiah is coming (he who is called Christ), when he comes he will show us all things" (Jn 4, 25). That profession had its counterpart in the title of his kingship nailed above him on the Cross, and professed by a Roman soldier in the last recorded human words at Calvary. "Truly this was the Son of God" (Mk 15, 39). His final gift to the Samaritan woman was the revelation of who he was. "I who speak to you am he." The sixth hour of Calvary was the manifestation of Jesus to the world. The King ascended his throne.

The invitation to drink and the promise of living water springing up to eternal life made to the Samaritan woman was repeated by Jesus in his solemn proclamation in the Temple on the Feast of Tabernacles. "If anyone thirst, let him come to me and drink who believes in me. As the Scripture said, 'out of his heart shall flow rivers of living water'." (Jn 7, 38). Here again it is the thirst of Jesus for human hearts which reached its deepest intensity in his cry. "I thirst", on the Cross. Faith in him is rewarded by a thirst for him.

The Tapestry

The cry of thirst was an admission of the agony of his suffering, and a final act of humility by which he allowed himself to be offered a drink from those very hands which had nailed him to the Cross. But it represented also something more profound related to the whole plan of salvation. It is a central theme in a tapestry into which are woven the actions and words at Calvary. His cry signalled the moment of the completion of his work. "To fulfil the scripture." The moment had come when he could say that he had completed his Father's work. 'It is accomplished.' He had come to establish the Kingdom of God, and now that kingdom was publicly proclaimed, Jesus of Nazareth, Lord and Master of redeemed mankind. As he hands back his soul to his Father he was ensuring the permanence of the kingdom through the Spirit who would come, and whose life-giving energy would be released by his Resurrection.

He thirsted for the realization of the unity of his Church for which he had prayed so intensely at the Last Supper; and that unity would be symbolized by his tunic which was 'without seam, woven from top to bottom'. Even the soldiers had the sensitivity to leave it as one. "Let us not tear it." We can be sure that the cry of Jesus sprang from the sensitive longing of his Heart that his Church would not be rent apart; that to all succeeding generations he was saying, "let them not tear it".

Having handed the new People of God into his Mother's keeping his work was done. The Holy Spirit, his final gift to the Church, would keep open the fountain of living water that would ever flow from his pierced side, and would be a source of eternal life for all who would believe in him.

The Thirsting Heart

The deepest longings of every person have been described in Holy Scripture under the form of thirst. "My soul thirsts for thee; as in a dry and weary land where no water is" (Ps 62, 1). Like the heart panting for the fountains of water, the human traveller in his desert journey can be overcome by thirst unless, the Lord, who gives living waters, refresh him. In his unfathomable love God both creates thirst for himself in the human heart, and, at the same time, slakes that thirst. Jesus, forsaken on the Cross, does not abandon us to unquenchable thirst.

But we can do the two wrongs which the People of God committed. We can forsake him, the fountain of living water, and build for ourselves broken cisterns which hold no water.

How grave a wrong to forsake him who was forsaken for love of us. In a world strewn with broken cisterns we have to ensure that the cisterns of our hearts retain the fountain of his grace with which he wants to fill them.

The thirst of Jesus is an invitation to us to develop an ever deeper thirst for the truth of his redeeming love and of the gift of the Holy Spirit. Here is the summary of St. Augustine: "The Lord cried out to us to come to him and drink on condition that we would feel within us an interior thirst for him". Because he loves he gives us to drink; because we drink we thirst again.

12 Her finest hour

*When Jesus saw his mother, and the
disciple whom he loved standing near,
he said to his mother, "Woman, behold,
your son!" Then he said to the disciple,
"Behold, your mother!" And from that
hour the disciple took her to his own
home.*

John 19, 26, 27

JESUS loved his own until the end. Among his disciples whom he called his own was Mary who was his first disciple. And as his love followed them until the end, so also did his Mother and her love remain with him until the final moments of his life. The love she gave him at Bethlehem she offered him at Calvary.

As in all his childhood needs she had been

close to him, so, in that moment she was near him. In that supreme moment of his suffering his Mother could not bear to be absent. In the hour of total abandonment, when he looked around for someone to comfort him, he found the companionship of his Mother.

Until the end of time the pathos of that scene —the Mother standing in majestic grandeur beside her dying Son — will be dwelt on and described by saints and christian artists. Amid the orgy of hatred that surrounded the dying Saviour there stood his Mother with Magdalene and John. This trinity of persons were the world's noblest lovers and the world's most attentive listeners. When so many walked no more with him on his final journey, they were faithful until the end. Like three characters in a great drama, each had a distinctive role in the drama of redemption.

Magdalene, who, in a gesture of profound love had once washed his feet with her tears, deserved to be at the Master's feet at the end. Her tears expressed the wordless love-song of repentant love. She was the mourner enduring the long sorrow of an aching heart.

It was the unique privilege of John to be allowed to come close to the secrets of the heart of Jesus. As on the first occasion when he met the Master and stayed with him that day, so he stayed with him on the day of Calvary. He had known the experience of leaning on the Master's breast at the Last Supper, and of recording the outpouring of his love on that night; now beneath the Cross he was to be again the sole recorder of the breathtaking words that fell from the Saviour's lips; words, so few but priceless in content they form a unique revelation of the hearts of Jesus and Mary.

The Testament

Pope John XXIII often used to say that if we want to understand Mary we must find her in the moment of the testament. The title he used for describing the spiritual motherhood of Mary was 'the testament of the dying Jesus.' He felt that we have not often enough repeated and reflected on the words, 'Behold your Mother,' "the last testament of the Lord who, in the supreme moment of his life donated his Mother to the world as the universal mother of all who believe in him and form his holy Church."

In the moment when, in the final outpouring of his love, he offered his life to his Father, he bestowed on the whole human family the gift of his Mother. She received her mission, which she accepted with the same readiness as she had accepted the Divine Motherhood. The "Fiat" of Nazareth reached its completion at Calvary.

Even in the midst of the deepest anguish of her life there began a deep and new joy, that of a mother rejoicing in her new children. Just as the Incarnation and the saving love of Jesus are always new, so her motherhood was beginning once more, a living again through all the ecstasy and wonder of Bethlehem. In the darkness of the cave she had welcomed her new-born son; in the gloom of Calvary she gazed with wonder and joy on her new family. In that, her finest hour, began a motherhood that will go on till the end of time.

From there also began her new pondering of the word; she gathered "all these things" and treasured the precious memories and mysteries of the Cross to hand on to her children.

Mary's pondering of the word was not simply a nostalgic memory of the past; she was and remains the strong woman entering with an intense activity of faith and love into the mystery of her Son, setting herself to the day-to-day task of caring for him with a calm industry. Just as she had taken him from the Crib and faced the road into exile, so on Calvary she folded the whole human family in her strong maternal embrace, and set out on the road again, a pilgrim mother with a pilgrim people. As the side of her Son was opened , so also her heart was opened to become a source of inexhaustible love for her new family. Then she became the Woman whose hour had come, the hour of the beginning of a new motherhood. She became the Woman standing on the globe, as she was seen by St. Catherine Labouré with the light and redeeming grace of Christ flowing from her hands. Two hearts as one, the Hearts of the Son and Mother. United in a martyrdom of suffering, they radiate a new impulse of love towards the whole family of the redeemed.

On the Road

Mary does not simply stand on the globe. She walks with her children. In a phrase of Pope John Paul II, "Mary walks with the Church and the Church walks with Mary." The first to enjoy her companionship on the road was John. "The disciple took her to his own home" (Jn 19, 27). He became her first adopted child. The Mother and son on the road together; history was repeating itself in a new form. Another hidden life, Mary sharing with her new-found son the many ineffable secrets and experiences of the love she had given and received from Jesus; the many intimacies that had passed between Mother and Son; the many memories recalled of their shared prayer of twilight and the bliss of many sunset hours together. The Mother who had carried the Saviour at her breast, and the disciple who had leaned on the Master's breast had both felt the heart-beat of his tenderest love. In the first exercise of her new mission the beloved disciple became the beloved son of the Mother of Jesus.

But the span of her embrace has no limits. The heart of Mary beat with the heart of Christ; it is in his Heart that we discover the greatness of his Mother. And, like the inexhaustible riches of his love given whole and entire to every person, so she gives to each of us the totality of her maternal love. Each of us shares in it and all have it completely.

She lavishes on all of us what is noblest and loveliest in human motherhood; the sensitivity that interprets our deepest needs. She who stood by the Cross does not stand afar off when we are in pain or in trouble. There is an instinct in us to reach for the clasp of her hand, to rush to her arms when we are in danger. There is a cry that comes to our lips, as Hilaire Belloc put it,

Mother of God, and Mother of me,
Save me alive from the howl of the sea.

She had devoted herself to the mystery of salvation serving the Person and work of her Son (*Vat. II The Church);* so she now, as Mother of the redeemed, devotes herself to bring to us the fruits of salvation and reveals to us the wonders of his mercy which she had experienced at Calvary.

Rich in Mercy

This thought has been beautifully presented by Pope John Paul II in his Encyclical, *"Dives in*

Misericordia," "No one experiences as did the Mother of the Crucified Lord the mystery of the Cross . . . thus Mary is the one who knows in depth the mystery of divine mercy . . . in this sense we call her Mother of mercy . . . she has been deputed in a special way to bring close to men that love which he came to reveal.

"This revelation is specially fruitful, because it is founded on the Mother of God, on the singular touch of her maternal heart, on her particular sensitivity and capacity to reach out to all those who are more ready to accept the merciful love of a mother. this is one of the greatest and most vivifying mysteries of Christianity.

"We have every right to believe that our generation also was included in the words of the Mother of God when she glorified the mercy 'from generation to generation' shared in by all who allow themselves to be guided by the fear of the Lord."

These striking words are a reminder to us that the Lord who is rich in mercy has bequeathed to us his Mother, who dispenses to us the inexhaustible riches of his loving mercy; and that Mary enters into every event, every hope and heartbreak of our lives, with all the tenderness and power of the mother's love that she gave him. If we take her to our own home she will surely make us her own.

13 Heart ever open

*But one of the soldiers pierced his side
with a spear, and at once there came out
blood and water. He who saw it has
borne witness – his testimony is true,
and he knows that he tells the truth –
that you also may believe. For these
things took place that the scripture
might be fulfilled, "Not a bone of him
shall be broken." And again, another
scripture says, "They shall look on him
whom they have pierced."*

John 19, 34-37

WITH such intense love did God love
the world that he sent his only Son
to save the world. That great love drama reached
its climax when his Son handed himself back into

his Father's hands as he was about to die on the Cross.

In that solemn moment man perpetrated his final act of violence on his Redeemer, opening his side with a spear. In the Liturgy of Holy Saturday the Canticle which greets the risen Lord sings of the "happy fault" which won such a Redeemer. It was a happy sword thrust that opened the side of the Redeemer, thus releasing a fountain of life and making visible the love that prompted him to die for us.

St John rounded off his description of the final moments of Jesus on the Cross by recalling two prophecies. "Not a bone of him shall be broken." "They shall look on him whom they have pierced." That look was not merely with the external eyes of the body — it was the interior look of faith which penetrated the mystery. The Evangelist was allowed to come so close to that mystery for a special purpose, that through his testimony we might be able to open our eyes in faith. "He who saw it has borne witness — his testimony is true and he knows that he tells the truth — that you also may believe." Sublime truths related to sublime events. The moment of prophecy was over; now it was the great reality. Man had been redeemed in the Blood of the Lamb; the whole human family is responsible for the piercing of the Saviour.

Human eyes might try to turn aside, and not look face to face on him who had looked with compassion on us; but there is no way that human hearts could disown involvement. The personal, individual love with which his heart overflowed when he delivered himself for me deserves the individual acknowledgement of my share in his death for my salvation.

The Final Epiphany

The opening of the side of Jesus opened also a vision of his heart wounded by sin. It was his final Epiphany, the manifestation to the nations of the wonders of his merciful love. His pierced side became at once the source of a fountain and a doorway of access. "At once there came out blood and water." In that moment the Church was born; she came forth from the heart of Jesus bearing gifts; water that would cleanse and create a holy people through Baptism; blood which, in the Eucharist, would sustain life, and Mary, who would be a mother to the Church on her pilgrim journey.

St John, who had leaned on the breast of the Lord, and felt the heartbeat of his love, looked on his pierced side, and through that loving gaze he saw the glorification of the Saviour.

From the earliest moments of her existence the Church has been led by the Holy Spirit into an unending pondering on the Heart of Jesus; she is ever entering the gateway of his pierced side into an adventurous exploration of the depths and riches of love within his Heart. She fixes her loving gaze on his pierced side, and sees it as the doorway of the great temple, and listens again, in the setting of Calvary, to the words he had spoken in the Temple on the Feast of Tabernacles: "If any one thirst, let him come to me and drink who believes in me. As the Scripture has said, 'Out of his heart shall flow rivers of living water'."

Calvary was the fulfilment of all prophecy, of all the promises of God to cleanse mankind from sin, and to reveal the face of his mercy through the Heart of his Son in all the tender intimacy of his love. As God's people, wearily trudging their way through the desert, parched with thirst, were given a sign of God's care when water gushed forth from the rock, so God's new people, created on the Cross, will ever come, weary from the road, to find at the fountain of his Heart the refreshment of living waters.

Gift to Each

The divine gift is offered to every person. "If any one thirst." It is sufficient to believe that this man is the Son of God and that, through his blood there is forgiveness of sin, and that through the Paschal Mystery there comes the Bread of eternal life.

It was a gift offered in the moment of the deepest suffering, yet through the darkness there was already beginning to sound the song of rejoicing. Not a bone of the paschal lamb was broken; now the Lamb of God, offering himself on the Cross is accepted by his Father, and "the Lamb who was slain is worthy to receive power and wealth and wisdom and might and honour and glory and blessing" (Rev. 5, 12). In that glorious moment the new redeemed people became the spouse and bride of the Lamb, and thus the solemn alliance was completed.

In the moments before he died Jesus expressed his merciful love in words of tender forgiveness. No sooner had his lips closed in death than his Heart was opened, and for all times his Heart ever open would proclaim the compassion of his forgiveness, and his readiness to refresh all who are weary and heavy laden.

Final Destination

The road that we have followed in these reflections has brought us to our final destination — the heart

76

of our Saviour. Through various moments of special tenderness we saw a sudden, even if momentary, flash of his merciful love; but now as we reach the gateway of his Heart the full splendour of his love, the glory of his infinitely lovable Person with all the marvels of his divine and human love, bursts upon us. It is the moment when Tabor and Calvary become one, when, having come, we want to stay. St. Bonaventure puts it so beautifully. "When once we come to the Heart of our Lord it will be no easy task to tear us away, since it is good for us to be here."

We become part of that great company that crowds the roadway to his Heart. Just as he had stood by the lakeside and looked with compassion on the multitudes surging towards him, bringing with them the blind and deaf and crippled, so, now that he has given the supreme proof of his love on the Cross, do the peoples of the world surge forward towards him with ever greater urgency and hope.

Each of us who looks with compassion on the Crucified is drawn irresistibly towards him. The Holy Spirit, whose sanctifying energy was released by his Resurrection, lights up the mystery of his redeeming love, and warms our hearts to an ever more generous response of love for him.

Invitation to All

The Heart of Jesus, ever open, is an open invitation to us to open our hearts. His invitation to us to come carries the certainty of reward. "To his open heart the Saviour invites all men to draw water with joy from the springs of salvation" *(Preface,*

Mass of the Sacred Heart). Coming to the Heart of Jesus, we taste the joys of his victory; we experience the serene calm of his risen life. Our day-to-day living is often a battle against all the hazards and fears of a storm-tossed voyage. To enter the heart of Jesus is like reaching the still waters of a quiet haven from a stormy ocean.

But within his heart we find more than the experience of passive response; we are drawn into a great rhythm of the ceaseless activity of that communion of life between the Father, Son, and Holy Spirit. We are caught up into a great song of praise, thanks and glory. And, as well, we are rediscovering the boundless love of Jesus for all men.

So, as we come close to him whom we have pierced, we are moved to an ever more intense offering of repentant love. "He was wounded for our transgressions, he was bruised for our iniquities" (Is 53, 5). To make amends to him we have much to do. St Bonaventure gives us a perfect formula of prayer:

"Let us pray that the Sacred Heart may deign to wound our heart, still so hard, still so impenitent, and bind it with the bands of his love."

14 The Empty Tomb

Mary Magdalene, and Mary the mother of James and Salome . . . on the first day of the week went to the tomb when the sun had risen.

And entering the tomb, they saw a young man sitting on the right side, dressed in a white robe; and they were amazed. And he said to them, "Do not be amazed; you seek Jesus of Nazareth, who was crucified. He has risen, he is not here; see the place where they laid him.

But go, tell his disciples and Peter that he is going before you to Galilee."

Mark 16, 1, 2, 5-7.

When the darkness settled down on Calvary all seemed ended. Soon the body of Jesus was in the tomb which was securely closed and guarded. The thirst for his blood had been satisfied, and the fury of his enemies, like a spent storm, rumbled off into silence as they drifted from the scene.

But the friends of Jesus did not forget their absent Lord. A kind of grey silence enveloped that night and the Sabbath day that followed. Through the long sorrow of aching hearts, the hours, so filled with grief, moved slowly. Each of those clouded hours must have seemed to them an eternity.

But love is ever active and those whom Jesus loved, and who had loved him until the end, did not drift through those hours in a numbed, hopeless regret. We can glimpse through those curtained hours and see how they filled the emptiness with compassionate love. His own, who had fled when their Lord was seized, did not abandon him. We are told of their tears. "They mourned and wept." (Mk 16, 16). We are not told of his Mother and John, who must surely have fulfilled, in that dark moment, the mission to care for her which he had just received from his dying Lord. With the same serenity that marked their bearing beneath the Cross, they shared, in some quiet corner of the city, a dialogue of wordless grief. The women, who, also, had been with them beneath the Cross, prepared to express their final, tender gesture of service to him. They bought ointments and spices to anoint his body.

Silent Victory

Then a simple gospel phrase, "when it was early on the first day of the week", ushered in the dawn of the happiest day in the world's history, the first day of the new world, the world of universal hope. Before the world awoke from sleep the Lord had risen. Just as he had come in the silence of the night, unnoticed, so he rose in the silence of the day of salvation, unseen by human eyes. He who had been lifted up in derision on the Cross was raised up in glory by his Father. Thus was the exaltation of Jesus completed in his resurrection, and the glory of his victory over death and sin gives meaning to the Cross. Death, resurrection, glory, were not just a sequence of events; they were the plan of God, his loving design to liberate us from sin and bring about our final exaltation, our entering into a new life, his own glorious life. "Let all the house of Israel know assuredly that God has made him both Lord and Christ, this Jesus whom you crucified." (Acts 2, 36). The combat that began in the stillness of Bethlehem was completed on Calvary. No clash of swords signalled his victory, but only the silent thrust of the sword that pierced his side. It was in the inner sanctuary of his Heart that the battle was won, and it was fitting that he would emerge unnoticed from the tomb.

The Chosen Few

The last page of the salvation drama is as fascinating as the first. The song of angels heralded his first coming and invited a chosen few to greet him; chosen because they were the poor of heart whose hearts were open to receive him; and, having given him the gift of their adoration, they went back across the hills praising God. There was sweet music too in the voices of angels announcing his final victory. "He is not here, he is risen as he said . . ." And again it was the few coming to offer him love, fragrant as their precious ointments, who were chosen to hear the good news, and to rush through the roads of the world to communicate the message across the span of centuries till it reached us in the now of our lives. Pope John Paul II sums up the marvel of that moment. " 'He is risen'. We repeat the words with simplicity because they come from people of simplicity. They come from hearts that love and that have so loved Christ that they are capable of preaching nothing else but the truth about him."

The urgent impulse of love is never deterred by obstacles. "Who will roll back the stone?" the women said: but neither the stone nor the guards prevented them from coming to the tomb.

They were quickly rewarded with the gift of vision and hearing. They saw a man standing with "appearance like lightning and his raiment white as snow." Women who had grieved to look on the blood-stained garments of their Lord were now amazed and gladdened by a vision radiant, which, even before they received the message, spoke of joy and newness and renewal. An angel had been the first to receive the message of the Incarnation; and God used the ministry of angels again to communicate the news of the resurrection of Jesus.

Mary Magdalene and the other faithful women, who had come to perform a service of reverence to the body of the dead Saviour, were given a new mission to become messengers of the news of his resurrection. They were given this stupendous privilege, not merely as a token of his friendship but that they would be the chosen witnesses of his resurrection. Standing round the empty tomb, they became the first community of witnesses, a miniature assembly of the Easter Church. Before they were given the vision of the risen Lord their eyes were opened in wonder before the dazzling vision of the angelic figures at the tomb.

They had looked on him where men had laid him on the Cross, and now they were told to look at the place where they laid him in the tomb which now became the symbol of his victory.

No sooner did they receive the message than they were given their mission. "Go quickly and tell his disciples that he has risen from the dead" (Mt 28, 7). Like Mary, rising with haste from Nazareth, they hurried to tell the news to Peter and the disciples, with something of her springtime joy in their hearts. "So they departed quickly from the tomb with fear and great joy, and ran to tell his disciples" (Mt 28, 8).

To die with Christ and to rise with him by the power of his resurrection is the programme of our christian life. We are ever being invited to enter into the paschal mystery; to allow ourselves to be caught up into the rhythm of those great mysterious events of his sacred passion, death and resurrection. Each week-end of our christian life is meant to be a re-living of Good Friday and Holy Saturday, as we prepare to celebrate with great joy the eternal day of Easter in our Sunday Mass.

Holy Saturday

In that paschal drama, Holy Saturday has a particular charm. It is truly a "Preparation Day", when, in the blessed company of the friends of Jesus, we weep and mourn and wait with patience for the new day of the Lord. The faithful women of Galilee have much to teach us. They wept for their absent Lord; but they did not grieve like those who have no hope; their hearts were turned towards him in silent adoration.

A writer of the Eastern Church has beautifully described the charm of Holy Saturday. "While Jesus is in the tomb is a time of waiting and of silence; a time for secret life, hidden and contemplative, near him, with him. Holy Saturday is the feast of those hidden lovers whom the world is unaware of, and who wish to be known only by Jesus."

Holy Saturday is the meeting-place of mourning and hope. It is partly turned towards the Lord's tomb, and partly towards the risen Lord. Our attention and our hearts are with the Lord in the tomb as we mourn his going; but the splendid sunshine of his Easter dawn is always drying our tears.

15 Garden of Easter

Mary Magdalene . . . turned round and saw Jesus standing, but she did not know that it was Jesus. Jesus said to her, "Woman, why are you weeping? Whom do you seek?"

Supposing him to be the gardener, she said to him, "Sir, if you have carried him away, tell me where you have laid him, and I will take him away."

Jesus said to her, "Mary." She turned and said to him in Hebrew, "Rabboni!" (which means Teacher).

John 20, 14-16.

THERE is a particular charm about the description of the Resurrection in St John's Gospel. It is like a drama centred round three persons, Mary Magdalene, Peter, John. These ardent lovers of Jesus expressed, by words and actions, their intense longing to find and possess their Lord. They were drawn irresistibly towards the tomb in which he had been laid.

They had no other strength but love; and that impulse is full of power. "Love is strong as death" (Cant 8, 6). They could remember his words. "The days will come when the bridegroom is taken away from them" (Mk 2, 20). Now that day had come, and the bridegroom had gone, leaving a void in their hearts.

Drama

Then, with the coming of a new day, "on the first day of the week" the drama begins to unfold. Mary Magdalene is on her way to the tomb to perform the final gesture of love, the anointing of the body of her Lord. The mood suddenly changes. Like a ray of sunlight coming through a dark cloud, there is a sense of a smile breaking through tears, a mood of breathless excitement. In that dawn, when the bridegroom returned, everyone is running. Mary Magdalene is running; Peter is running; John is running. Love always runs, rushing to a presence, to an embrace. One quick look at the tomb, and when Mary Magdalene "saw that the stone had been taken away from the tomb, she ran and went to Simon Peter, and the other disciple, the one whom Jesus loved." This news sent Peter and John hurrying to the tomb. "They both ran, but the other disciple outran Peter and reached the tomb first."

At this point of the story we are in the presence of courtesy, both human and divine. John waited to allow Peter enter the tomb before him. The disciple whom Jesus loved deserved to be among the first to receive the news of his Resurrection, but

Peter, the disciple whom Jesus chose to be the chief shepherd of his flock, was to be the first of the apostles to see him. "He appeared to Cephas, and then to the twelve" (1 Cor 15, 5).

Now Mary Magdalene became the key figure in the drama. All that she does and says has a profound meaning. Having seen the empty tomb "the disciples returned to their own homes." But it was left to a repentant sinner to stay. Mary could not be drawn away. A heart that loved with such intensity could find no home at a distance from her Beloved. "Mary stood weeping outside the tomb, and as she wept she stooped down to look at the tomb." She looked twice. St Gregory the Great explains why. "A soul that loves is never satisfied with a single glance — the power of love urges it to continue seeking. Mary had already sought and found nothing. But she persevered, and therefore found the object of her love."

When she entered the tomb she repeated to the two angels what she had already said to Peter and John, expressing her intense pain of loss. "They have taken away my Lord, and I do not know where they have laid him."

Quietly as Dawn

Then, as she turned around, the risen Jesus stood before her in the garden. Ever so quietly, like the first rays of dawn stealing across the land, the Light of the world came forth. His coming was so leisurely, with such unhurried pace was the unfolding of the revelation of his Resurrection. With a whole world waiting for the Good News, he was content to give his whole attention to one repentant sinner. It was again the divine care of the one, as if there were no one else in all the world needing his personal attention. The first recorded words of the risen Lord were to bid a woman, and not only her but all humanity, to dry its tears. "Woman, why are you weeping?"

"Whom do you seek?" The same words that he had addressed to a hostile crowd in the darkness of Gethsemane were now spoken to an ardent lover in the clear light of a new dawn. She, like them, sought Jesus of Nazareth, not to lay violent hands on him but to hold him in an embrace of love.

Supposing him to be the gardener, she said to him, "if you have carried him away, tell me where you have laid him, and I will take him away". No need for Mary to mention his name. "He" alone was the object of her search, the only one who counted in her life. Enough for her to have him, and in that possessive impulse of the lover, she would take him away, away once and for all from the hands of men.

Called by Name

"Jesus said to her, 'Mary'." In the moment when she did not recognize him he proved to her that he recognized her. One word was enough; in a flash she knew his voice. Her eyes had deceived her, but her ears were attuned to every nuance of her Lord's voice. It was by hearing that she learned that the Lord had risen. It was thus fitting that she who, in silent mourning at the foot of the Cross, had remained in contemplation of the mystery of his saving love, should be an early witness of his Resurrection through the hearing of his word.

Jesus, addressing her by name, not only manifested to her the fact of his resurrection, but also the intimacy of his love for her. The Good Shepherd knows his sheep by name. "The sheep follow him for they know his voice" (Jn 10, 4). Magdalene had followed him to Calvary, and beyond, drawn irresistibly towards him.

One word from Jesus was enough for Mary; one word from her summarised the rush of faith and love which flooded her soul in the joy of recognition. "Rabboni." It conveyed the idea of the greatness of him whom she looked to as her great One, her only One, the One to whom she owed all she knew, to whom she had given all she had.

While he gave her the privilege of an individual personal meeting, he told her of his new mode of life now beginning. So she must learn to leave behind her accustomed way of expressing her affection, by resting at his feet. He has to complete the drama of his glorification. "I have not yet ascended to my Father and your Father." In that moment she received a new mission. Mary, the contemplative, longing to worship at his feet in silent adoration, became Mary, "apostle of the apostles," hurrying to bring the news of his Resurrection to them. "Mary Magdalene went and said to the disciples, "I have seen the Lord" (Jn 20, 18). This message, expressed in so few words, changed, not only the lives of the apostles but the whole course of history.

Garden of Easter

The message of Magdalen has an impact on our own personal lives. She says to us, as she said to them "that the Lord had said these things to her." The Lord who invites us to keep vigil with him in Gethsemane, and to stand close to him at Calvary, invites us also to meet in the garden of Easter. There he is ever coming forth from the tomb granting us the joy of a personal encounter. In the garden of Eden God walked with man in the quiet of evening in the intimacy of a loving encounter. But sin brought separation and tears. Only in the garden of Easter was that joy restored when the risen Lord, in the quiet of morning, walked with us again, bringing with him a message of life and joy and bathing our lives in the splendour of his Resurrection.

Maybe he comes when the anguish of living and the torment of burdens too hard to bear leave us in tears. Meeting him is always a new dawn, and to us also he says, "why are you weeping?" Cardinal John Wright aptly describes the joy of the meeting. "The Garden of Easter is remembered with joy. There are no evils so saddening, nor troubles so trying that christians who remember Easter cannot sustain with hope. All gardens have been given new beauty by the remembrance of the garden of Easter."

In the garden of Easter all tears are dried. And our Faith, through the habit of attentive listening, makes us alert to the very tone of his voice; we are able to recognize him when he calls us, as he called Magdalene, by our first name. For us also, one word of greeting is enough. "Rabboni."

You are the One who cares; you are the One who counts for me.

16 Memories and Dreams

*So they drew near to the village to
which they were going. He appeared to
be going further, but they constrained
him, saying, "Stay with us, for it is
toward evening and the day is now far
spent."*

*When he was at table with them, he
took the bread and blessed, and broke it,
and gave it to them. And their eyes were
opened and they recognised him; and he
vanished out of their sight. They said to
each other, "Did not our hearts burn
within us while he talked to us on the
road, while he opened to us the
scriptures?"*

Luke 24, 28-32.

How noiseless, how calm, how
imperceptible are God's ways of
revealing his mighty deeds! So much of his
immense work of salvation done in silence,
sometimes in secret.

The key moments in the drama of Redemption involved descent and ascent, and in each there was the same unnoticed, noiseless action of God in his mightiest mysteries of power and love. The descent of the Son of God in becoming man was unperceived "like the dew falling on the fleece. When all things were in silence, and the night was on its way, your Divine Word came." (Christmas antiphon).

So, also, was his ascent from the dead, his Resurrection, which was the crowning mystery of his whole saving plan, and which was to change the whole course of history. That mystery took place in a similar silence, and, in the calm of Easter Day, was, almost casually, made known to a mere handful of people. In the serene peace of the garden in the early morning the resplendent light of his risen life played on the eyes of a few friends who had kept on believing and loving him until the end. Like the morning sun filtering through the mists of dawn he opened their eyes to the full glory of his victory.

All of that band received a mission, either to become messengers of the news or witnesses to strengthen the conviction of faith in the mystery of the Resurrection. Never did so few receive so sacred a message destined for so many. And each time there was the joy of the risen Lord to show himself to so few, there was the seemingly limitless time he was prepared to give them.

The Road

Calm as the morning of Easter Day, so, also, was the evening. A garden; a road. Magdalene mourning with uncontrolled tears; two men burdened with broken hopes and shattered dreams setting out from Jerusalem. They left a city bathed in sunshine, but their vision was still obscured with the darkness of Calvary. The deepening shadows of evening played on their road; the dusk was settling down on Emmaus, their destination, and there was only the gloom of blighted hopes in their hearts.

The very tone and subject of their conversation betrayed the cause of their gloom — the nostalgic longing for a material kingdom on which they had set their hearts. As they walked they were joined by a stranger. "The Lord joined them," said St Bede, "in order to enkindle in their minds faith in his Resurrection, and also, to fulfil his promise 'Where two or three are gathered together in my name, there am I in the midst of them' " (Mt 18, 20).

It would seem as if Jesus caught up with them from behind, almost like a friend's hand on one's shoulder, making us aware of his nearness. They expressed no surprise at his presence; their only surprise was when he entered into conversation and asked what things they were conversing about. That there could be anyone in Jerusalem who was unaware of the extraordinary events of those last days left them stupefied. They were rooted to the ground in baffled silence. "And they stood still, looking sad."

Ever so gently by a series of questions, just as he had done with the woman at Jacob's well, he led them on to an inner vision and conviction of faith. "What is this conversation?" "What things?" (Lk 24, 19). They opened out into an account of what had happened; and the key word of their story was "we had hoped he was the one to redeem Israel" (Lk 24, 21).

When eyes are fixed on earthly horizons the vision of the eternal is dimmed.

Salvation History

Now it was the turn of the stranger to speak; and with that endless patience he had so often shown to the apostles when they were immersed in their petty wranglings he gave them a full lesson in salvation history. The Pasch has a past, a present and a future.

The death of Jesus was not the dashing of hopes; it was the building of life. "Was it not necessary that Christ should suffer and so enter into his glory?" It was thus that men would receive the full impact of his redeeming love.

Along the glorious road from Moses through all the prophets he took them. How marvellous a Liturgy of the Word! "He interpreted to them in all the scriptures the things concerning himself" (Lk 24, 27). He took them back along the road of memories. The interpretation of the scriptures with which he had opened his ministry in the Synagogue of Nazareth now reached its completion in the quiet of an evening conversation on a leisurely walk to an unknown village. By the time he had brought their minds up to that present moment they were convinced of a burning in their hearts. The yesterday had touched the today of their lives. Truly it could be said of that dramatic moment. "This day a scripture has been fulfilled in your midst" (Lk 4, 21).

The Paschal Mystery has a forward impulse; it is always drawing us towards a great moment ahead. Memories make hearts to burn; and burning hearts awaken dreams of having him and desires of not losing him in any future stretch of the road.

The words of Jesus prepared the hearts of those two men for the final revelation. They, who had been slow of heart to believe, became quick to believe.

Stay

One word of welcome was enough. "They constrained him", saying, 'stay with us for it is towards evening and the day is now far spent'." Surely a phrase that must take its place as one of the most sublime expressions in the whole Gospel. It tells him of their longing; the nostalgia for him; the unendurable loneliness of living without him.

The readiness of his acceptance more than matched the eagerness of their invitation. "So he went in to stay with them." From that moment he took the initiative. "When he was at the table with them he took the bread and blessed, and broke it, and gave it to them." And in a sudden flash they recognised him; and before they had time to fall at his feet, he had vanished from their eyes. He had given them a whole evening to themselves. He had completed a Paschal revelation to them. It was enough.

That dusty path through the hills which was covered in shadows when they started out, was suddenly illuminated by a divine light that lit up the mellow tints of evening. For two men the details of the whole story fell into position. The unfolding of the scriptures, the burning of hearts, and then their recognising him in the breaking of bread.

That dusty road to Emmaus, how different it

must have seemed to those men whose eyes now lit up with the splendour of the risen Lord, their hearts now aglow with a new love. The experience was enough for a life-time. They had enjoyed the companionship of him whom Pope Paul II called "the Divine Pilgrim among pilgrims". And as they returned to Jerusalem to tell the news to the eleven they were travelling through evening shadows, but the glow of Easter morning was in their hearts.

Final Moments

The final moments of the story are so full of charm, told with a few delicate words like touches from the brush of Rembrandt that complete the picture.

First, as they reached the place to which they were going their unrecognised companion seemed to be going farther. It is a trait so often found in Jesus. He allows us such freedom. He does not intrude upon us as an unwanted guest. He is prepared to stand at the door and knock. He leaves the invitation to us. And so it was that evening at Emmaus. But men whose hearts had become aglow could not endure parting company with him, even though, as yet, their eyes had not been opened.

Well-Trodden Path

The road to Emmaus is a well-trodden path. It can be that aimless winding path through the hills that we have all set out at some moment or another when all the plans and dreams in which "we had hoped" had gone up in flames, and Emmaus offered no solace.

But then the Stranger joins us, and, as for two disillusioned men, Emmaus becomes a Tabor when it is good to be with the Lord who opens our eyes.

Every Eucharist celebration is, in a real sense, an Emmaus, the Lord opening our hearts to the Scriptures and our recognising him in the breaking of bread. Emmaus is but a halting-place, a little village on the road to the City where the Lord will sit down with us and there will be no evening. Pascal has the lovely thought, "We would not go on searching for him if we had not already found him".

Stay with us, Lord, so that we may go on finding you each new time with a new love in our hearts.

17 Closed Doors

*On the evening of that day, the first day
of the week, the doors being shut where
the disciples were, for fear of the Jews,
Jesus came and stood among them and
said to them, "Peace be with you."*

*When he had said this, he showed
them his hands and his side. Then the
disciples were glad when they saw the
Lord.*

*Jesus said to them again, "Peace be
with you. As the Father has sent me,
even so I send you."*

John 20, 19-21.

It is a strange paradox that the divine
Son of God in his coming into the world,
to embrace and take possession of human hearts,
was welcomed by closed doors. "There was no
place for them in the inn" (Lk 2, 7). And when the
final drama ended, man tried to lock him away,
placing a mighty stone to guard his tomb, lest his
few friends should try to take him.

But neither the crowded inn nor the lonely

sepulchre could impede his urge to reach human hearts. A lovely Antiphon of the Christmas Liturgy describes the divine paradox of opening and closing. "O Key of David and Sceptre of Israel, what you open, no one else can close again, what you close no one can open. O come to lead the captives from prison; free those who sit in darkness and in the shadow of death."

In order to free all captives and dispel all darkness he came forth from the tomb, victorious over death. The door of the tomb that enclosed him was opened, and would never enclose him again; the darkness of the tomb was dispelled by the light that would ever shine forth from it.

The great duel between life and death had been fought and won. The stone had been rolled back, and Jesus, the eternal dominator of death had emerged, and could walk any road, and join any company. Having travelled the road to Emmaus, he made his final recorded journey of Easter Day to join his apostles at Jerusalem.

Despite the news that had reached them of his resurrection, and even though Peter had already seen him, the shadow of fear and disbelief still hung over them. The little flock whom he had specially chosen, and made to be with him, and who had shared the marvel of the Eucharist with him, had, within hours, abandoned him, and "they all forsook him and fled" (Mk 14, 50). When the shepherd was stricken the flock was dispersed; but their failure was a breakdown in courage, not of love; and when the shepherd had triumphed, they re-assembled.

Men, haggard and weary, with the effects of a terrible ordeal visible on their faces. Apart from John, they all shared a common memory of abandonment of their master. And yet, they must also, even in that moment, have retained memories of many of those great moments of his compassion when he had sent a repentant sinner on his or her way, rejoicing, with the words "your sins are forgiven; go in peace".

And then, as they were listening to the two disciples, returned from Emmaus, recounting their recognition of him in the breaking of bread, he suddenly stood among them. The account gives a sense of the centrality of Jesus. He who had become, and would remain, the centre of their lives, stood in the centre. No word of reproach for their failure; but with the same majestic calm that he had shown when he confronted the storm on the lake, he quietened their troubled hearts. A simple gesture of his hand, one soft-spoken greeting — "Peace be with you" — was enough to remove the fears and questionings that had arisen in their hearts.

Few Words

The recorded words of the risen Jesus are few, but they are so rich in content. The first words that were spoken to his apostles on his last appearance on Easter Day, were more than a greeting: they expressed the conferring of a gift, that gift that he had promised them on the night of the Last Supper. "My peace I give to you . . . let not your hearts be troubled" (Jn 14, 27).

St Augustine throws a light on the beauty of that moment. "The lord greeted his disciples, saying: "Peace be with you". This indeed is peace and the salutation of salvation; for salutation receives its name from salvation. And what better than that salvation itself should greet mankind.

"He rose from the sepulchre, and though his wounds were healed the scars remained. For this he judged expedient for his disciples, that he should keep his scars to heal the wounds of their souls."

The inmost recesses of their troubled hearts were flooded with the gift of his Easter peace, a peace that would never again desert them. The fears that had gripped them would never again afflict them, for the Holy Spirit was about to come to them to give them courage so that they would flee no more from him; and open their eyes so that they would never again mistake who he was. He opened their minds so that they would for ever be clear on the purpose of his mission, and on the nature of their own future mission. The importance of that moment was, not so much that they would realize that he had a real body, as they saw him eat bread, but that they would recognize and believe the mystery of his Resurrection.

They Shall Look

To complete his description of Calvary, St. John had quoted the prophet Zephaniah. "They shall look on him whom they have pierced" (Jn 19, 37). Now, as the risen Lord stood among them, these men could look close-up on him, whom they, and all humanity, had pierced. Not only did he open their eyes to see his wounds, but he opened their minds to the inner conviction of his Resurrection. They were the first to whom he showed the marks of his wounds. They have no words now; there was just the silent looking of repentant lovers. It was left to Thomas, at a later moment, to put into words the sublime expression of faith and adoration. "My Lord, and my God."

Apostolic Mission

Having calmed their troubled hearts with his first salutation of peace, he repeated "Peace be with you"; but this time his words were part of the mission he was giving them — to be messengers of peace to all the world, a peace that would be the fruit of his Resurrection.

This was a moment of supreme importance. It was the moment when they were constituted into the official community of witnesses of his Resurrection. For St Luke, it was the point of departure of their apostolic mission when they received their commission, and the Good News of Christ's victory was on its way, "beginning from Jerusalem". For St John, the apparition of Jesus to his apostles marked the conclusion of his account of the Paschal Mystery.

All the other apparitions of Easter Day converged on this point. It was for the apostles to be, above all, witnesses and preachers of his resurrection. When they wanted to fill the vacant place in their ranks, they said, "one of these must be witnesses with us of his resurrection" (Acts 1, 22).

Paschal Age

It was the beginning of the paschal age: the dawn of the new creation. As the Spirit had breathed over the waters in the first moment of creation, now, the risen Lord completed the re-creation of a fallen world by breathing on the apostles the life-giving power of his Holy Spirit by which the Church would make human souls spring to new life and be flooded with the peace of his risen glory in the Sacrament of Penance.

One among so many facets of this lovely scene captures our attention. How often is it not repeated in our own lives? In moments when we have betrayed him by sin, do we not tend to lock ourselves away from him; and in our fear or shame, are almost fearful of meeting him. And when we do summon enough courage to come to ask his pardon, he comes into our presence with a greeting rather than a reproof. "Peace be with you." What seemed an ordeal becomes so easy when the risen Lord stands before us, and we experience, in the words of Pope John Paul II, "the personal encounter with the crucified and forgiving Christ." He asks so little and he gives so much. Enough for us to tell our sins to a Priest and ask for pardon, and the risen Jesus has healed our wounds, and filled our souls with his paschal joy. He who is gentle of heart acts gently with hearts that need to be restored to his love. So quietly, as with the apostles, he re-enters our lives, and we recover the companionship of his love and presence, as if nothing had happened.

In the sacrament of his pardon, we meet him in the serene calm of Easter Day. So quietly he comes. The therapy of his healing love is so painless. How relaxed his bearing with his apostles: how he puts them at their ease! "Have you anything to eat?" So also with us. It is like the relaxed gathering of friends at table.

A writer of the Eastern Church has caught the atmosphere of that moment. "Right away Jesus is going to resume his place at our table and share our life again. That will come about in an instant; but as far as we are concerned it must be done in humility and repentance. The exterior attitude will be simple and easy. Yet it must be characterised by an interior prostration."

While we rejoice in his peace we must remember his wounds, and bow, in loving adoration, before the love that saved us.

18 Springtime again

So they departed quickly from the tomb with fear and great joy, and ran to tell his disciples. And behold, Jesus met them and said, "Hail!" And they came up and took hold of his feet and worshipped him.

Then Jesus said to them, "Do not be afraid; go and tell my brethren to go to Galilee, and there they will see me."

Mt 28, 8-10

HE who is the Way leads the way. Thus it was for the apostles from the moment Jesus crossed their path for the first time. The very form of his invitation indicated that he would lead the way. "Come, follow me". It was for them to follow after him along the paths he had chosen.

Often the Gospels describe him as walking ahead. "And they were on the road, going up to Jerusalem, and Jesus was walking ahead of them"

(Mk 10, 32). That was a solemn moment when he took the road to Jerusalem on his way to Calvary. "Behold we are going up to Jerusalem" (Mk 10, 33). For the apostles it was an invitation to follow, and a revelation of the paschal mystery. He told them "what was going to happen to him" (Mk 10, 32).

Going Before

Scarcely had Jesus risen when there is mention of another journey, another "going before" his disciples. The women, coming to the tomb, had no sooner arrived than they were sent on their way. Father Léon-Defour makes this apt observation. "They have scarcely been invited to look at the place where Jesus lay, when they are asked to leave. Like a springboard which repels whoever puts his weight upon it, the tomb pushes them away from itself. It symbolizes everything that remains of the life of the earthly Jesus." So, also, the message they received sends the apostles on their way to a new finding of Jesus, a new vision of him in all the glory of his risen life. For men who had lost heart, Galilee would become the land of hope.

The women, arriving at the tomb, together with the news of his resurrection, received a message from the angel to convey to the apostles. "Go, tell his disciples and Peter that he is going before you into Galilee; there you will see him as he told you" (Mk 16, 7). A second time the risen Jesus himself repeated the message which contained, also, an invitation. "Go and tell my brethren to go to Galilee, and there they will see me" (Mt 28, 10).

Paschal Journey

These men who had seen the loving plan of

redemption unfold in Galilee, saw it completed in Jerusalem. Now they were invited to make a paschal journey back to Galilee; and their visit would be rewarded. "There you shall see him." It was important for them to see him, for it was his purpose that they would be the official witnesses of his resurrection; and so we find much of his attention in his risen days given to them, putting the final touches on his preparation of this little group of men for their mission to proclaim the mystery of his resurrection to the whole world.

So different from their reluctant following of Jesus as he went to Jerusalem to suffer and die was this journey into Galilee. Now they were aware of the supreme proof of his redeeming love revealed to them by his shedding of his blood. They had come close to what Pope John Paul II calls "the burning furnace of the paschal mystery".

Their hearts must have burned within them as they travelled up through the hills. Men who had run to the tomb must have hastened. Mary had come with haste down through the hill country, bringing the Redeemer to be greeted with great joy as she crossed the threshold of her cousin's house. Now it was a journey with an equally joyful haste, crossing the threshold of a new world to greet the risen Redeemer.

Springtime

Once he had invited them to come apart to rest a little when he saw them fatigued. Now, more than fatigue burdened them. They had been through the terrible ordeal of Calvary; guilty of abandoning their Lord; they had lived through a long night when they mourned and wept for their absent Lord.

They arrived in Galilee in full springtime. So often Jesus had used the hills and lake and calm silence of the open spaces to illustrate his message. Now the apostles, leaving behind them the memories of darkness and earthquakes and the howling of frenzied mobs, came into Galilee, whose calm and freshness were symbols of the peace and refreshment they were about to experience. Entering Galilee Jesus brought with him the freshness of the springtime of a new world. All nature exhaled the freshness of springtime; this was but a pale shadow of the newness of life which the risen Lord brought to a faded world.

Greeting his apostles in Galilee Jesus imparted to their hearts a mood of springtime. It must have been for them what we would call a kind of renewal course, a return to the fervour and joy of those first blessed days when he had made them to be with him. It was a place of treasured memories of the excitement and intimacy of the first call to follow him, the ecstasy and generosity of their first response. They had left all things to follow him. Now they had found all they would ever need to see and possess — they had found the risen Jesus.

There were memories of his first preaching of the kingdom; of those parables he had used in Galilee that spoke of seed-time and fields ready for the harvest. The lilies were again in bloom which once he had used to show how the exquisite care his heavenly Father had devoted to fashioning even "one of these" was only a shadow of the personal love of his Father for every person.

Deeper Reason

But, perhaps, there was also a deeper reason for his

inviting them to Galilee. "There you will see him." There they saw him in the glory and power of his victory. There they now saw how his miracles of healing were woven into the tapestry of redemption, which was his supreme work of love. At Cana of Galilee they had witnessed the first of his signs, and "his disciples believed in him" (Jn 2, 11). Now they had seen the final sign, the sign of the Cross, the sign of the empty tomb that spoke of his final victory over death and sin. It was thus a moment of a deepening of their convictions, a refreshment of love.

Our Galilee

There is something for all of us in this story of the journey of the risen Jesus into Galilee. We can make our own, as addressed to ourselves, the words addressed to his apostles. "Behold he goes before you into Galilee; there you will see him." None of us but at some moment has had our Gethsemane and Calvary; an ordeal in the darkness of a seemingly never-ending night; a burden too heavy to bear; a project that has gone astray, leaving us desolate with our blighted hopes. Maybe there has been betrayal and abandonment of the Lord whom we had once promised to follow until the end.

In such a moment of our lives there is a Galilee we all need. We need to meet the risen Lord who will restore us in the springtime freshness of Galilee. He is always ready to give us the invitation he gave to his apostles. It is, for us, as for them, a return to sources, a reviving of precious memories of his call to follow him, of that first finding of him, and how we "stayed with him that day" (Jn 1, 39) in the intimacy of a personal companionship. "There you will see him." We see him in that inner vision of faith where he speaks to us again his "Come, follow me," in the eternal today of the gospel. There, in the full power of his victory, he speaks to all the storms that beset us as he once addressed the turbulent waters of the lake. "Be still, and there was a great calm" (Mk 4, 39).

This is the Galilee of the soul to which he walks before us, and where he waits for us, to calm our troubled hearts, and confer on us the calm of his Easter peace.

A monk of the eastern Church has recaptured the beauty of that moment. " 'He will go before you into Galilee . . .' My child, you will not have to evoke my presence painfully. I shall be faithful to the appointment which I made with you. I shall do more than wait for you in this Galilee of memories. Now I go before you. I shall lead you there. When your heart is once again fixed on Galilee, the One who is guiding you will make himself known to you, and he will speak to you . . ."

In the anxieties, fears, problems that press in upon us we need to set our gaze fixedly on the risen Jesus, and to return often to the Galilee of his risen days.

19 His risen days

*After this Jesus revealed himself again
to the disciples by the sea of Tiberias;
and he revealed himself in this way.
Simon Peter, Thomas called the Twin,
Nathanael of Cana in Galilee, the sons
of Zebedee, and two others of his
disciples were together.*

*Simon said to them, "I am going
fishing." They said to him, "we will go
with you."*

John 21, 1-3.

WHEN the risen Jesus joined his
disciples in Galilee it was high
springtime. Spring conveys a message of newness;
of a kind of resurrection in nature; new flowers,
opening out their petals to the sunlight for the first
time, are a symbol of the beauty of new life. But the
coming of Jesus into Galilee was more than a
coincidence with nature's springtime. He was the
bringer of new life; he heralded new times for a new

world, in which all humanity, through the power of his resurrection, became a new creation.

He had left the empty tomb behind for ever; the linen cloths, folded in the corner, had no further purpose. He walked resplendent in the newness of life.

"The winter is past . . . the flowers appear on the earth, the time of singing has come" (Cant 2, 11, 12). The winter of the cross had passed, and unlike the rhythm of nature's seasons, it would not return. So, there remains the eternal song of his victory. The flowers appear; they are the qualities of his risen life, whose fragrance fills the world with paschal freshness. Unlike nature's flowers that fade, they remain eternally in bloom.

Two Histories

Galilee, in the life of Jesus, had two histories. It recalled memories of fatigue when he fell asleep in a boat at the end of a day's work. There was the sorrow of rejection by his own people; when hands could touch him to push him over the brow of the hill. He who had come to make a home among men found no place to lay his head.

But after he had risen, a different history began. No longer fatigue, no more hunger; and, even when he did eat, it was only to assure his disciples of the reality of his resurrection.

As the lake, when its waters are still, is a clear reflection of skies and hills, so the paschal calm in the heart of Jesus gave a perfect reflection of new facets and expressions of his holiness that characterized his risen life. The Church, in her Liturgy, invokes him through his "holy resurrection". She presents his resurrection as illumining his holiness in a particular way. "The death he died, he died to sin, once for all, but the life he lives he lives to God" (Rom 6, 10). Now he has shaken off dependence on all human things; he is utterly free from weakness. He had finished the work his Father had given him to do. He had drunk the chalice; he had endured the cross; his side had been opened, from which a new people, redeemed in his blood, would ever draw waters with joy. For the glory of his victory he now addresses his Father with a new prayer of thanks and praise.

Abbot Marmion has beautifully described the new mode of life of the risen Jesus. "Now that his sacred humanity is set free from all necessities, from all the infirmities of our earthly condition, it yields itself more than ever to the glory of the Father. The life of the risen Christ becomes an infinite source of glory to his Father, there is no longer any weakness in him; all is light, strength, beauty, life; all in him sings an uninterrupted canticle of praise." With the fullness of paschal joy in his heart, Jesus sang a new canticle of praise and love that resounded in the hearts of the apostles and echoed not only through the hills of Galilee, but, till the end of time, will continue to resound in every avenue of human life, and in the silent depths of human hearts that are prompted to live to God.

Shared Gift

Just as his resurrection was not for himself alone, so his paschal joy was a gift to be shared, and the first sharers were his apostles. Paschal joy is a permanent quality of his Church, a most sacred gift to every member of his people. Through his holy Resurrection, in each of us is verified his prayer to his father, "that they might have my joy fulfilled in themselves" (Jn 16, 7). His joy is not a superficial mood, that slips from us as quickly as it comes; it creates a well of peace and calm at the still centre of our hearts that cannot be ruffled by the storms or pains of life.

A feature of the newness of the life of the risen Jesus was his coming and going. He was in their midst; and suddenly he was gone. His apostles lived in the experience of his surprises. Just as people fell back in amazement in the presence of his miracles, now the very sight of him was enough to fill human hearts with joy. "The disciples were glad when they saw the Lord" (Jn 20, 20). They lived in the wonderment of discovering and rediscovering their Lord. So often, seeing a figure, and then a sudden flash of recognition, they exclaim, in an outburst of joy, "It is the Lord". Those were spontaneous expressions of joy from those who knew how much their Lord had suffered. The source and centre of Christian joy is always found in the mystery of the Cross.

The Church keeps the Cross of Jesus ever before our eyes to stimulate our sorrow, and to enliven our love of our crucified Lord, but she also lives in a most serene joy, which is the fruit of his suffering and resurrection.

Eternal Youth

Paschal joy keeps the Church young, and so she moves from the springtime of her first days, not towards winter, for the Lord dies no more, but towards the new springtime, the new advent,

114

which Popes of our time see ahead of her as she faces another millenium.

As the early Christians gathered round the table of the Lord with "glad and generous hearts" (Acts 2, 47), so would the Church invite us to find, in the paschal mystery, an unending source of purest joy. "I will go to the altar of God, who gives joy to my youth" (Ps 42, 4). Once we allow the paschal joy of Jesus to flood our hearts, he keeps our lives full of his surprises, ever joining us on the road, giving us companionship on our pilgrim way; ever bursting through our closed doors, dispelling our hidden fears and easing our secret sorrow, ever standing on the shore, waiting to greet us.

Because he has given us his Holy Spirit we are able to live our lives in the mood of springtime, and the flowers appear; they are the gifts of joy, love, peace, which remain ever in bloom in our hearts.

New Each Day

Our whole Christian life is meant to be a daily experience of the joy of the risen Lord. No day but he delights us with a new surprise, and the deep and recurring surprise he gives us is his mercy, which is a daily source of amazement for us. "His mercies come new every morning" (Lam 3, 3).

Cardinal Pironio perfectly expressed how the risen life of Jesus is meant to influence our daily lives: "Easter is a serene and deep invitation to joy . . . to prolong the paschal mystery in our lives is to make transparent and contagious the joy of the risen Lord."

Joy is not meant to be locked away in our hearts. It is, by its nature, contagious. After the three disciples had seen the Lord shine like the sun on Tabor they came down, seeing nobody but "Jesus only" (Mt 17, 8). From that moment, in every face, in every event, on every roadway they saw nobody but Jesus only; and thus they relived the wonderment and joy of that moment.

The risen Lord gives us the grace to radiate his joy, and to find him anew in every person and moment of our daily lives. His joy is for sharing; and so, every family, every religious community, is meant to be a paschal community, whose members radiate joy to one another, and keep on finding in one another a new feature of the risen Jesus every day, and thus they remain always young in the newness of Jesus.

Our world has lost its sense of wonder; and not even the feverish search for novelties and distractions can relieve the prevailing boredom. We could fall victims to boredom and fatigue with living unless we are immersed in the joy of the paschal newness of the risen Jesus, who, through his cross and resurrection, makes all things new. Otherwise, we could grow old before our time. Because he has given us the newness of life he has refreshed our hearts in love, and so we can sing every day a new song which is a canticle of joy.

A final word from Cardinal Pironio: "If each day is not new for us, we grow old in our work, in personal relationships, with those with whom we live, in our own Christian existence, in our priestly ministry or our consecrated life."

What if we, each day, could make a kind of springtime journey through Galilee where we might meet the Lord in the unfading freshness of his risen days!

20 An Easter Dawn

Just as day was breaking, Jesus stood on the beach . . . That disciple whom Jesus loved said to Peter, "It is the Lord!"

When they got out on land, they saw a charcoal fire there with fish lying on it, and bread. Jesus said to them, "Bring some of the fish that you have just caught."

So Simon Peter went aboard and hauled the net ashore.

Jesus said to them, "Come and have breakfast." Now none of the disciples dared to ask him, "Who are you?" They knew it was the Lord.

Jesus came and took the bread and gave it to them, and so with the fish.

Jn 21, 4, 9, 12, 13

THERE was one dawn that had a special splendour; it was the dawn that broke over Galilee to greet the risen Lord. "Just as the day was breaking, Jesus stood on the beach." The rising sun saluted him who is the Dawn.

He stood alone. So short a time since he was alone on the Cross, and there was darkness over the whole earth. Now all nature, the rising sun, the lilies of Galilee were out to greet him. The beauty of the dawn was only a pale reflection of the resplendent beauty of the risen Lord, and of the new day of salvation, which, through his death, had dawned on the world. This was the morning that would have no evening in the eternal day of the Church.

He had promised his apostles that they would see him in Galilee; so, true to his promise, he waited to greet them as they pulled in to shore after a night's fishing. Once before he had come to them shortly before the dawn, on a night when the wind and the waves were against them, and they were distressed in rowing. On this morning they had not lived through distress, but they were dispirited, tired, hungry; a whole night's work fishing a lake they knew so well, and yet "that night they caught nothing".

As they came close to the shore they saw a figure standing on the beach. As in the garden, and as on the road to Emmaus, so also on the lakeside, their recognition of the risen Lord was gradual. Magdalene recognized his voice; but here, not even his voice revealed him to his disciples. When he spoke "Children, have you any fish?", they did not yet recognize him. He was to teach them by a sign. "Cast the net on the right side and you will find some". So they cast it and now they were not able to haul it in for the quantity of fish. At Emmaus it was a sign of the bread; on the lake it was the sign of the fish. In a flash, they recognized him. "That disciple whom Jesus loved said to Peter, "it is the Lord!" " The reaction of Peter was as spontaneous as John's cry of joy. "He sprang into the sea" to reach the shore immediately to greet his Lord.

Abundance

In this lovely scene we are in the presence of the divine abundance, which was a sign that the messianic era of salvation had arrived. John was the disciple who had tasted love in abundance; and through his gospel runs the theme of the prodigality of divine abundance. There was enough wine at Cana; for the hungry multitude on the hillside there was sufficient; "so also with the fish, as much as they wanted" (Jn 6, 11). The promised living waters would issue from a fountain that would never dry. Who ever would drink, "would never thirst" (Jn 4, 14). Love would never come to an end; neither would the life that would have its source in life-giving bread. "I came that they may have life and have it abundantly" (Jn 10, 10).

On that morning in Galilee Jesus was giving his apostles the final lesson. His side, opened on the cross, became an unending source of life. These fishers of men would learn from the overflowing net the inexhaustible fruitfulness of the mission which he would soon confide to them.

Breakfast

His disciples learned another lesson on that blessed morning: that he who dispensed inexhaustible riches also has a care for the smaller needs. While he was filling their nets, he was also condescending to meet their need of a morning meal. "They saw a charcoal fire and fish". The hands that had been fastened to the Cross and were extended from east to west to embrace a fallen world, could descend to gather fuel for a fire and prepare a meal.

On a solemn night they had been invited to sit at table with him and to take and eat. Now in the informal setting of a lakeside they received another invitation "Come and have breakfast". And the exquisite detail, he served it to them. "Jesus came and took the bread and gave it to them, and so with the fish". The Lord washing feet, serving a meal; in those touches of divine condescension he showed how love can be expressed through tender attention to the smaller needs. His disciples were no longer in doubt of his identity. "They knew it was the Lord". As men had recognized him in the breaking of bread on the evening of Easter Day, now he was recognized in the serving of bread. The hands that served them bore marks easy to see.

The whole scene breathes that serenity and stillness that characterized all the appearances of the risen Lord. An ancient homily for Holy Saturday says: "Today there is a great silence over the earth, a great stillness because the King sleeps; the earth was in terror and was still because God slept in the flesh". On this morning by the lakeside there is also silence, but of a different kind; it is the stillness and the calm in once troubled hearts, because the King lives. That reassurance and peace that Jesus brought to his disciples in his appearances must surely have strengthened them against distress or gloom when the full fury of a pagan world would break on the infant Church.

St. Gregory the Great gives us another insight into this lovely moment. "What ever does the sea represent other than the present age that expends itself in a turmoil of quarrels on the surging waves of transitory life? But the solid shore — is that not a figure of the land of eternal rest?" Jesus stands on the shore, secure and calm, in the certainty of his victory. His gaze was turned towards his apostles, while he allowed them to experience failure, but ready to give success to the work of their hands.

Back-Drop

We can penetrate the beauty of that moment, and make it a starting-point for a reflection on the gift of the Holy Eucharist. It is easy to relate it to our Sunday Mass. On that day we set out to greet the risen Lord. It is a kind of pulling in to shore, while the fretful uneasy rhythm of daily work slows down. Like the apostles, returning after a night's work with nothing to show for their labours, so can our week often end in frustration. There is something in the stillness of the christian Sunday that recalls the calm of the lakeside on that morning in Galilee when Jesus stood on the shore.

He stands on the shores of our lives, not merely a spectator of our daily struggle. His activity on our behalf never ceases. He who was preparing a meal for his disciples while they toiled on the lake, is ever providing for us the life-giving meal of the Bread of Life to sustain us.

The joy of the apostles, their eagerness to greet him is the same paschal joy that every celebration of the Holy Eucharist brings us. The Mystery of Faith refreshes our faith, which brings us to the moment of recognition, when we too cry out with joy, "it is the Lord".

"Come and have breakfast". The invitation given to the apostles is issued to each of us in the eternal present of our lives. The feast is always ready; there is the joy of being chosen guests. "Happy are those who are called to his supper". The Divine Host is ever active on our behalf, providing for us the food that will make us one day share with him the heavenly banquet in the morning of eternity that will have no evening.

To be worthy of his invitation requires a constant deepening of faith and love.

21 Towards Pastures Green

When they had finished breakfast, Jesus said to Simon Peter, "Simon, son of John, do you love me more than these?"

He said to him, "Yes, Lord; you know that I love you." He said to him, "Feed my lambs." A second time he said to him, Simon, son of John, do you love me?" he said to him, "Yes, Lord; you know that I love you." He said to him, "Tend my sheep."

He said to him the third time, "Simon, son of John, do you love me?" . . . and he said to him, "Lord, you know everything; you know that I love you." Jesus said to him, "Feed my sheep."

Jn 21, 15-17.

BEFORE ever Peter met Jesus he showed a readiness to follow him. When his brother Andrew came to tell him the good news, "We have found the Messiah," he brought him to Jesus (Jn 1, 41, 42). The marvel of that encounter is one of the loveliest moments of wonderment in the Gospel. A man, in all his rugged simplicity and honesty, brought into the presence of the Lord, ready to offer himself and leave all things to follow him. "Jesus looked at him" (Jn 1, 42). When Jesus looks, it is never a mere casual glance; it is the looking with love that penetrates to the heart. Love has eyes. That day Jesus, looking at Peter, drew him irresistibly to himself. There would be another moment when Jesus would look on Peter, and that look melted his heart, and he went out and wept bitterly for having denied his Lord.

The first recorded journey of Peter was a pilgrimage of Faith that brought him into the presence of Jesus for the first time; and the childlike faith of this cheerful giver was accepted. The Lord made him his own; gave him a new name and a special mission.

Ready to Love

Peter had a heart ready to love. In a later moment when the Heart of the Saviour was saddened by the loss of friends who walked no more with him, the assuring words of Peter brought him consolation. "Lord, to whom shall we go? You have the words of eternal life; and we have believed, and have come to know, that you are the Holy One of God" (Jn 6, 68, 69). The man who had been chosen to lead was ready to give the obedience of faith. "At your word I will let down the nets" (Lk 5, 5). It was for Peter, the great lover, to be also the great believer, and to formulate the sublime act of faith in the divinity of Christ, upon which the

Church was founded. "You are the Christ the Son of the living God" (Mt 16, 16). This solemn profession of faith was the fruit of a special revelation by the Father.

Heart to Heart

Now on the lakeside the risen Jesus placed the seal on his choice of Peter. There took place a dialogue whose charm and beauty will still be fresh when the world has grown old. It was heart speaking to heart; love's question, prompting love's response. At Caesarea Philippi it had been the profession of faith; on the lakeside it was the profession of love, Love, in its most sublime expression, needs few words. Three simple questions that went straight to the heart, and three equally spontaneous replies that came straight from the heart. "Simon, son of John, do you love me more than these?", and the immediate reply, "Yes, Lord, you know that I love you."

Just as the Father had revealed to him the divinity of his Son, so, on this occasion, the Father must have opened his eyes to see the heart of his Son, worthy of a total outpouring of his own heart, in a spontaneous response of love. Peter's love was so childlike and unconditional, the very thought that his master should require further assurance by asking a third profession of it, grieved him. Surely, the Lord, whose knowledge was as all-embracing as his love, should require no further proof. "Peter was grieved because he said to him the third time, 'Do you love me?' And he said to him, 'Lord you know everything; you know that I love you'" (Jn 21, 17).

In his threefold profession he more than made

amends for his threefold denial of his Lord. St Augustine links those two contrasting moments of Peter's history. "It became his mission of love to pasture the Lord's flock, just as it had been a sign of fear to deny the shepherd."

Jesus had built his Church on Peter's faith. Now he rewarded Peter's love by placing his flock in his arms. "Feed my lambs; feed my sheep." The man who had enough strength in his arms to haul ashore a net full of large fish would have arms strong enough to hold the flock of Christ, and to keep them secure in his tender embrace.

Final Revelation

"Feed my sheep." These words, which are among the last recorded words of the risen Jesus, are a summary and completion of the revelation of the inexhaustible love of the Heart of the Good Shepherd. In that solemn moment they must have recalled to Peter memories of the shepherd themes, so vividly depicted by the prophets; and also opened up to him a picture of the mission of shepherding that lay ahead of him.

Through centuries of waiting, God has revealed his saving love under the image of the shepherd; the intimacy of his love; his carrying the lambs in his arms; the daily care, finding ever fresh and green pastures for his flock. In Jesus, the Good Shepherd, the image became the reality. The songs of shepherds, announcing tidings of great joy, in the birth of him who is called Emmanuel, God with us, told the world that the God who cares had sent his Son as the Good Shepherd, who would have a personal, intimate care of every person, till the end of time

In the glorious tableau presented in St John's gospel, he is depicted as the shepherd who knows each sheep by name; who searches out the lost sheep till he finds it, and brings it back rejoicing. There is the description of the reciprocal current of love between shepherd and sheep; a bond, so intimate as to be a reflection of the love-current between Father and Son. "I know my own and my own know me, as the Father knows me, and I know the Father" (Jn 10, 14, 15).

There is no sounding the depths of the good Shepherd's love. He not only protects and feeds and rescues his flock from danger; he gives the final proof by laying down his life for his sheep. The same shoulders that had borne the lost sheep also bore the Cross from which he returned rejoicing, carrying the whole flock of the redeemed to his Father.

Peter's Experience

Peter had an intimate experience of the love of the Good Shepherd. He had been known and called by name; he had been pastured with the Bread of Life; and he had seen the shepherd stricken, and had become, for a time, one of the flock that was scattered. On that morning by the lake the scattered flock regrouped; and in the companionship of a meal served to them by hands that bore the marks of the wounds, the words of Jesus must have vividly come back to him. "'I will strike the shepherd and the sheep of the flock will be scattered; but after I am raised up, I will go before you into Galilee'. Peter declared to him, "Though they all fall away because of you I will never fall away'" (Mt 26, 31-33). Peter knew that his sin was forgiven because he had loved much, and because he was loved much.

This gospel moment had a particular importance, for it marks the beginning of a new world. "Feed my sheep" is another word for mercy, for the Lord's merciful, caring love providing for all future generations. The shepherd could not depart without arranging that the inexhaustible riches of his love would be available to every person till the end of time. As Jesus loved his own until the end, so would he commission his own to be shepherds in his place, and through them his sheep would be fed until the end, until the end of all loving.

Dietrich Von Hildebrand gives us a delightful summary of the beauty and importance of this moment. "The appeal to the love of Peter reveals the unfathomable mystery that Christ seeks our love, that he wants not only to be obeyed but also to be loved." His words "breathe an ineffable meekness and gloriously tender love, and in the divine 'Feed my sheep', there trembles the love for all those who have followed him, for all those who will ever follow him."

In the dialogue by the lakeside on that historic morning Jesus wrote the history of the Church, and, as well, the history of each of us. To all of us is posed the question which is also the divine pleading for our love. "Do you love me?" And as his love comes new every morning, so does his request for our response. As he humbled himself on the Cross for us, so does he humble himself in begging from us the love he so richly deserves. With something of the candour and childlike sincerity of Peter in our hearts can we not also make his reply our own? "You know that I love you." Would that our profession of love might always have about it the newness and beauty of that Galilean dawn!

22 The Divine Mandate

*Now the eleven disciples went to Galilee,
to the mountain to which Jesus had
directed them. And Jesus came and said
to them, "All authority in heaven and
on earth has been given to me. Go
therefore and make disciples of all
nations, baptizing them in the name of
the Father and of the Son and of the
Holy Spirit, teaching them to observe all
that I have commanded you . . ."*

Mt 28, 16-20.

Two words, "Come" and "Go", are like
a frame which encloses the history of
the apostles and their mission. So brief and yet so
deep in meaning. Jesus never wasted words.
When, at the beginning of his public mission, he
went out to find partners, his eyes rested,
seemingly at random, on a few men. He came upon
them without warning, as they were immersed in
the routine of their daily work. To each he gave a

personal, definite call. "Come, follow me." And, in every case, there was the same generous, unconditional response. No discussion, no request for time to think it over, with a half promise of coming, perhaps tomorrow. Today, for these men, was the now of history.

The Divine Lover is also a jealous lover, and nothing short of total possession of their hearts would content him. The magnetism of his love, expressed in his invitation to come and follow him, was enough to win them. With complete openness of heart, and without regret, they left a world behind them, and found a new world in Jesus. He never left them out of his sight. With exquisite care he fashioned them for their future mission. They became part of him. The very proximity of his presence was enough to set their hearts aglow. Every road they travelled with him, was, in effect, like a road to Emmaus — a road to new discoveries — as he unfolded the scriptures to them.

Formation Process

The Gospels give us a glimpse of the gentle process of formation by which Jesus prepared them for their final mission. In the flush of excitement after their first taste of preaching in his name they rushed back to him. He showed them their need to balance their apostolic journeys with a constant journey inward to the desert stillness of prayer. He bade them come apart and rest awhile. His purpose in gathering them round him to be with him was not merely for the joy of their companionship. He made them to be with him, in order to prepare them to go forth from him. "And he appointed them to be with him, and to be sent out to preach" (Mk 2, 14). He was constantly insisting on their attentive listening before they could become worthy speakers. "Let these words sink into your ears" (Lk 9, 44).

Then came the dramatic moment, when, shortly before his Ascension, he assembled them. St. Matthew places the meeting on a mountain of Galilee. As Abraham had gone with unquestioning obedience to the mountain of Moriah to which God had directed him, so the apostles "went to Galilee to the mountain to which Jesus had directed them".

Apostolic Mission

The joy of their taking the road with Jesus in the moment of the call reached its completion in the joy with which they now received their mission to take the road on his behalf, to radiate the paschal joy of his resurrection to a world then, and always, urgently needing the Good News. In this final appearance of the risen Jesus they received their solemn commission to go forth.

Simple and direct as had been the words which he had used to call them to follow him, was the formula with which he now gave them their mission. "Go, therefore, and make disciples of all the nations." "Go into all the world and preach the gospel to the whole of creation."

As these men stood on the threshold of a new world, Jesus opened out before their eyes the panoramic vision of the marvellous and mighty work that lay ahead of them. Limitless love has a universal embrace, opening out boundless horizons. The whole world was to be the object of their apostolic mission. At the Last Supper he had placed his Body and Blood into their hands, and their hearts had rejoiced; now he entrusted to their keeping the whole body of truth, the whole programme of life which he had received from his Father, and which they would hand on with joy to all who would believe and be baptised, and which would light up every road, and direct men's steps securely along the way to salvation.

They received their commission in springtime; and nature, clothed in its festive springtime dress, would remind them of the eternal freshness of the Gospel they were shortly to preach to the whole world. As the hills had echoed to the song of rejoicing in the coming of the Redeemer, so, as these bearers of the grace of Redemption were about to set out, the very hills would again burst into song. "You shall go out in joy, and be led forth in peace; the mountains and hills before you shall burst forth into singing" (Is 55, 12).

In that solemn moment when he was about to entrust to them the work of establishing his kingdom they bowed down in an act of worship. "When they saw him they worshipped him." But even in that moment there were some among them who still needed a strengthening of faith. "But some doubted." Jesus summoned the whole majesty of his divinity. "All authority in heaven and on earth has been given to me." So often he had reminded them that he had been sent by the Father; that he and the Father are one; that whoever looks on him sees the Father. The very love that the Father lavishes on his beloved Son, he bestows on these loved disciples of the Son, Intimate as the union of love was the union of truth; and the preaching of the apostles would ring true because it had the authority of authorship, which could be traced back through Jesus to the Father.

The Final Revelation

There was something majestic about the words of Jesus at this great moment. Words spoken on the Cross were the testament of the dying Jesus; words now spoken were the testament of the risen Jesus — his last recorded words; and so they deserve special attention.

Behind the majesty that flashes through them there is discernible also the throb of the heart of the Saviour. They represent the final revelation of his compassion. Once he had compassion on the multitude because they were scattered, like sheep without a shepherd. And the heart of the Good Shepherd responded to their need — to one of their deepest needs — the need for truth. "And he began to teach them many things" (Mk 6, 34).

The unfailing compassion of the Good Shepherd would be ever present to his flock through all future ages, exercised by shepherds who would be ever faithful to his solemn command, given at that moment. "Go into all the world and preach the gospel to all creation." Teach them "to observe all that I have commanded you". There would never be lacking in the Church what Pope John Paul II calls "Delegates of the Word". the panoramic sweep of his merciful love, stretching far as east is from west, would embrace every person.

The programme of life which the apostles were commanded to present was clear and precise. They were to baptize in the name of the Father and of the Son and of the Holy Spirit; and that sacrament would give to the baptized the light and strength to observe all things that he commanded.

Misson for All

There is a sense in which the words spoken to the apostles are meant for all of us. "Go into all the world." By our baptism we receive a gift of Faith to be shared, becoming bearers of light to a dark world, making an effective proclamation of the Good News by the wordless witness of our christian lives. Two successors of the apostles have given us valuable reflections which are relevant to the gospel moment when the apostles received their mission. Pope Paul VI, in his apostolic letter on the Evangelization of Peoples, says: "The Christian community is never closed in upon itself. The intimate life of this community —the life of listening to the Word and the Apostles' teaching, charity lived in a fraternal way, the sharing of bread — this intimate life only acquires its full meaning when it becomes a witness, when it evokes admiration and conversion, and when it becomes the preaching of the Good News. Thus it is the whole Church that received the mission to evangelize and the work of each individual member is important for the whole."

"Observe all that I have commanded you." Pope John Paul II emphasises the need to accept the whole Gospel, and that the person who wants to bend the truth to suit the lifestyle of our world is "like a spectator who gropes his way in a dark theatre, guided only by the usherette's flash light"

In the theatre of life where the intense drama of our lives is played, we need more than the tiny beam of the theatre usherette to guide our steps.

Well for us that the apostles, assembled on the mountain of Galilee, were faithful to their mission, and that the Church, speaking to us with the clarity and authority of the Divine Author of the Good News, makes it possible for us to walk always in the full light of the Day of Faith.

23 The Great Return

Then he led them out as far as Bethany,
and lifting up his hands he blessed them.
While he blessed them, he parted from
them, and was carried up into heaven. And
they worshipped him, and returned to
Jerusalem with great joy, and were
continually in the temple blessing God.

Luke 24, 50-53

THERE is in all of us an instinct to possess, or at least to long for the presence of one we love. This brings a tinge of pain to all goodbyes; and when the separation is final, or for long, the pain is all the keener. The parting of the ways, which is inevitably woven into our life's history, whether the parting is but for a while, or with the prospect of a longer absence, there comes the moment of leave-taking, the final embrace, the waving goodbye, the following with our eyes the direction of the loved one till he or she passes beyond our vision.

Jesus, sharing every human experience, except sin lived through moments of parting. There was the leave-taking of his Mother and of Nazareth as he set out, a homeless man on a lonely road, when his public ministry began. There came the moment, tinged with joy and sorrow, when he assembled his own to eat the pasch with them before he departed from them to suffer.

Then came the final farewell, the moment of his Ascension. As he had assembled them before he went to die, so he now gathered them before he went to glory. And, as always, he led them. "Then he led them as far as Bethany, and lifting up his hands he blessed them. While he blessed them, he parted from them, and was carried up into heaven". Thus took place the solemn liturgy of farewell. It was the moment of the great return. The Son, whose gaze had ever been fixed on his Father, having finished the work which his Father had sent him to do, now returned with joy into the eternal embrace of the Father who was always well pleased with his Son.

Uniqueness of Jesus

The uniqueness of Jesus that had filled the Gospels with his surprises now shone forth in the dramatic event which brought the whole paschal drama to its triumphant conclusion. His Ascension was not shrouded in the darkness of Calvary; it was bathed in the dazzling radiance of his final victory. It marked the culmination of all the fascinating surprises of the comings and goings of his risen days. It was a parting that was final, in that it brought to an end his visible presence; but it was completely unlike the parting of death. Cardinal Newman describes the leave-taking of death of loved ones, in a lovely phrase. "The silver cord of love is loosed. They have been followed by the vehement grief of tears, and the long sorrow of aching hearts". But through the risen days and appearances of Jesus there was woven a golden thread of unbroken joy; and for his disciples his going was not the loosing of the cord of love, but the continued experience of the long ecstasy of joyful hearts.

There is no one like Jesus, and there was nothing in human history to compare with his history, so full of dramatic contrasts. He who had experienced the desolation of abandonment now enjoyed the fulness of joy in his return to the eternal companionship of his Father. Men whose hearts he had won could watch him go without regret. Again, the words of Newman give us a beautiful analysis of that moment. "Now how was it, that when nature would have wept, the apostles rejoiced? ... There was no sorrow in the apostles, in spite of their loss ... for Christ surely had taught them what it was to have their treasure in heaven; and they rejoiced, not that their Lord was gone ... but that their hearts had gone with him".

Admirable Ascension

The Ascension marks the highest moment of his glorification. It is greeted in the Church's liturgy as being "admirable", which is another expression for the wonderment, the amazement, that is at the core of the Church's message, a perfect summary of the highest delight of the Good News.

The three disciples he had chosen to be with him on Tabor found it good to be there, even though they had only one shining moment of his resurrection radiance. Now, the penetrating vision of faith could pierce the cloud that hid him as he ascended, and they could share the joy of the whole court of heaven, in the song of welcome at his home-coming.

The shepherds, who had heard the song of the angels greeting his coming into the world, returned, rejoicing, across the hills. So also did the apostles, the appointed shepherds of the universal flock, "rejoice with exceeding joy as they returned to Jerusalem".

Together with the apostles, the whole of creation, the whole family of God until the end of time, will be ever bursting into song in an unending canticle of joy at the final glory of the risen Lord.

Not only does he carry with him the vivid memories of all the fatigue and pain and torment of human living, he took with him, also, the same compassion that he had shown on earth to all who were weary from the journey, and so he interprets all our deepest needs in his eternal intercession with his Father. But he does more; he carries us with him, in the sense that he focuses our longings, making us dwell by faith and hope and love, in our eternal homeland. He gives to our lives that forward impulse which keeps us pressing ever onwards. By this great mystery he expresses his love for us by refreshing us in hope, in opening our eyes to the lights of home, ahead of us. His Ascension keeps reminding us that the great realities are ahead; that this is but the world of shadows. Thus do we travel our pilgrim road, moving through shadows into light.

Our consumer society subtly advertises its

products as possessing the answer to all our dreams. It is a world ever promising but never fulfilling, and we need the powerful truths that are enshrined in the Ascension of Jesus to offset the allure of the world. Do we allow the stupendous reality of the Ascension to have its due influence on the day-to-day living and direction of our lives?

It has been said that life in heaven tends to be considered as a kind of postscript or appendix to a book, and that the drama of our earthly life supplies the text; whereas, the truth is the opposite. As an Eastern writer has put it, "our earthly life is but the preface to the book. Life in heaven will be its main text, and this text is endless".

Saint Gregory

In a homily preached in Rome on the feast of the Ascension, Saint Gregory the Great gave a sublime summary of the shape and sense of direction this feast should give to our lives. "With all our hearts we must follow Jesus where we know through faith that he ascended with his body. Let us flee earthly desires: none of the bonds here below satisfies us ... even if you are tossed on the waves of pursuits, cast the anchor of hope from today on the eternal homeland. Despite the weakness of our human nature, which still detains us here on earth, love attracts us to follow him since we are certain that the one who inspired such desire in us, Jesus Christ, will not disappoint our hope".

The sunlight of christian hope that brightens our lives does not mean that our road does not lead through many a dark tunnel and many a dark night of suffering. Jesus had no sooner vanished from the eyes of the apostles than they were reminded that they should not stand idly gazing heavenwards. "Why do you stand looking into heaven?" Life has to be lived, in all the humdrum and hazards and calvaries of daily living. But for those men who returned to Jerusalem rejoicing with exceeding joy, life would ever remain a "looking forward with holy hope".

Written in Heaven

For them and for us also, there remains the unshakable conviction that the Lord who promised to love on until the end, does keep on loving through this life and beyond. He who reigns on the Cross now reigns in glory. He has graven our names on his hands with the indelible seal of his blood. In returning to his Father he has carried with him the memories of our names and our needs. Words he once addressed to his apostles are true for all of us. "Rejoice that your names are written in heaven" (Lk 10, 20).

24 O Love Divine

When the day of Pentecost had come, they were all together in one place. And suddenly a sound came from heaven like the rush of a mighty wind, and it filled all the house where they were sitting.

And there appeared to them tongues as of fire, distributed and rested on each one of them. And they were all filled with the Holy Spirit and began to speak in other tongues, as the Spirit gave them utterance.

Acts 2, 1-4

THE love of Christ gathered the apostles into one. The same love that had assembled them for the Last Supper brought them together again after his Ascension. They were able to return with exceeding joy to that upper room where he had prayed for them, and where he had promised to send them another Paraclete, so that they would not be orphaned after he had gone from them. "All these with one accord devoted themselves to prayer, together with the women and Mary the mother of Jesus, and with his brethren" (Acts 1, 14). a blessed community of love, who, on the day of Pentecost, would become the Church, and, for all time, would be the model and inspiration of the Church at prayer.

Preparation

As for all the great moments of the salvation drama there was a preparation, a period of intense prayer; a kind of withdrawal into a desert stillness when hearts, united in a prayer of longing and pleading, waited with joyful expectation, for the promised Paraclete. As Jesus had been driven by the spirit (Mk 1, 12) into the desert, so these men and women were driven by a divine impulse, and welded into a union of praying hearts. It was a moment of total dedication to one purpose. "With one accord they devoted themselves to prayer."

Pentecost deserved such a preparation, for it would be the gathering together of the great themes of salvation, the beginning of a new world in the birthday of the Church.

Those who assembled had good reason to be part of that solemn exercise. It was fitting that Mary should be there, she who had opened her heart to every movement of the Holy Spirit. "The Spirit of the Lord has filled the universe" (Wis 1, 7). The Spirit of the Lord had filled the inmost recesses of her soul, making of her a temple worthy to give a home to the Redeemer. The Holy Spirit had lighted up every word and work of her Son; her soul glorified the Lord in his promise to send another Paraclete. Here was the prayer of intense pleading for the gifts of the Spirit on the Church, so that the harvest of the Cross would be a fruitful harvest on the coming feast of Pentecost. Mary's presence in the upper room linked two solemn moments of outpouring of divine love — the announcing and the fulfilment of the Good News. A phrase of Pope John Paul II has illumined those two events. "The Annunciation and Pentecost: here are two moments which are mysteriously perpetuated in the Church; what happened at Nazareth, what was done in the upper room, takes place each day on all the altars of the world; it is thus that the Spirit of the Lord has filled the universe." Mary, the apostles, the brethren, the women, formed a perfect communion of hearts. The petty disputes and dreams of earthly kingdoms no longer distracted the attention of the apostles. Their intense prayer expanded their hearts. The Lord Jesus, so generous in giving, had made them experts in generous responding, and so he loved them to the end by making them experts in love, worthy to receive the full outpouring of the Holy Spirit.

The munificence of the divine gifts is out of all proportion to human deserving. God so loved the world that he would send no one less than his beloved Son to save the world. The Son, in the final gesture of love on the Cross, allowed his side to be opened, so that the inexhaustible riches of salvation would flow from his Heart to all human hearts. The Holy Spirit completed the revelation of the divine outpouring.

Pentecost completed the marvel of the birth of the Redeemer; it consummated the glory of Easter. Jesus, on the Cross, embraced the whole human family; the Holy Spirit came as a gift to a whole assembly — to the family of the apostles, and to the great multitude assembled in Jerusalem, who, on the day of Pentecost, became the Church, giving to her a pentecostal and social holiness.

Language of Signs

The Holy Spirit expressed his power and holiness in the language of signs. At the wedding of Cana Jesus had worked the first of his signs. Now at the solemn wedding of the Holy Spirit with his Church, the coming of the Holy Spirit changed water into the wine of holiness — a never-ending supply for assembled guests who form the family of the Church. At Cana his disciples believed in him; at Pentecost his new-found disciples believed and were baptized.

The apostles were accused of being drunk with new wine; but it was the wine of the Spirit that made them aglow with the holiness and joy of the Spirit; and rather than confuse their words, gave them the ability to speak boldly and clearly the message of salvation.

There was the sound of a mighty wind. At the beginning of creation the spirit moved over the waters, and put shape and form on the primal chaos. Now came the re-shaping and re-creating, when the Spirit completed the redemptive work of the Son in restoring a fallen world.

There was the sign of fire. The Holy Spirit was the flame that purified and warmed the apostles, setting their hearts on fire with a new love.

Pentecost was an event entirely new and unique. It effected in the apostles an inner transformation that welded them into a new unity, making them the nucleus of the new christian community. There was a universal giving; the

Spirit rested on each of them. There was a univeral message that, through the gift of tongues, was intelligible to all; and so the dispersal and confusion of Babel ended once and for all; and every person could understand that the Son whom the Spirit of the Lord had anointed, had brought liberty to captives, the liberation from sin.

The Dove and the Lamb

At the baptism of Jesus, the Spirit descended on the Son. The Dove was turned towards the Lamb; and it is important for us to understand how the Spirit remains ever turned towards the Lamb, to manifest to the apostles and to all future generations, the power and invisible presence of Jesus, and his unending mission as Lamb of God to take away the sins of the world. The Spirit continues to manifest, through the Church, that there is forgiveness of sins through the Blood of the Lamb. So did the first preaching of Peter at Pentecost manifest the merciful love of the Son.

The day of Pentecost not only effected a radical change in the apostles: the Holy Spirit also brought about a dramatic influence on the great gathering in Jerusalem. Peter, standing with the eleven, lifted up his voice and addressed them. With a new courage he recalled to them the crime they had committed, and he made the first proclamation of witness to the resurrection on that first great day of the Church's life. "Jesus of Nazareth . . . you crucified and killed by the hands of lawless men. This Jesus God raised up and of that we all are witnesses." The Holy Spirit illumined their minds, and turn them towards the mystery of the redeeming love of Jesus. In that solemn day of conversion, God's word became a two-edged sword that pierced their hearts. "Now when they heard this they were cut to the heart, and said to Peter and the rest of the apostles, 'Brethren, what shall we do'?". They replied: "Repent and be baptized every one of you in the name of Jesus Christ for the forgiveness of your sins, and you shall receive the gift of the Holy Spirit."

Thus the Church began in a blaze of glory. Through the dramatic intervention of the Holy Spirit the great things of God were accomplished. Hearts of stone were turned into hearts of flesh. The very voices that had cried out "Crucify him" were now calmed. Those who had clamoured for his death now humbly responded to the invitation to repentance. Like the multitude on the mountain that had borne in upon him begging for bread, a new assembly now converged on the apostles, hungry for new life. "So those who received his word were baptized, and there were added that day about three thousand souls." The gift of the Holy Spirit is the final gesture of God's immeasurable love; and his permanent presence in the Church gives it a unifying and vivifying energy that forms a mighty shapeless multitude into a holy people.

To each individual person the Holy Spirit is constantly coming like the rustle of a gentle breeze. He is ever turning us towards the heart of the Saviour, enabling us to make each day a response of love to the merciful love which is ever cleansing us and making us worthy to enjoy the companionship of the Faith.

Every day of our lives is meant to be a Pentecost. But that presumes, on our part, a preparation. It means a habit of retiring to the upper room of our souls, not to shut ourselves away in lonely isolation, but to become part of that company that with one accord prayed together, awaiting the Holy Spirit at Pentecost. In the blessed company of Mary and the apostles, and united with their ceaseless prayer, we can await daily, with joy and certainty, the priceless gift of the Holy Spirit.

25 Beside the King

*Remembering the days of your lowliness
. . . beseech the Lord and speak to the
king concerning us and deliver us from
death.*

Esther 4, 8.*

MARY has left her footprints on many
roads. In the joy of springtime she
walked the road to Ain Karim to bring the Saviour
across the threshold of her cousin's home, the
same road that the Ark of the Covenant had
travelled on its way to the Holy City.

On a dark and fearful night she clasped her
Infant close to her heart as she faced the road into
exile. Having followed her Son during his public
life she travelled with him the final road to Calvary.

She had been one with him in her martyrdom
of heart. But the darkness of Calvary was not a
night without hope. She who was faithful till the
end did not need the strengthening of faith which
Jesus gave to his disciples through his recorded

appearances. But we can be sure that as he went before them into Galilee, Mary was there also, enjoying the serene calm of those joyful days, singing in her heart her Alleluia to her risen Lord.

As the apostles set out after Pentecost Mary was near them mothering the infant Church in the new Bethlehem of its infant days.

Love Requires Presence

But it was fitting that the Mother should soon be united with her Son in glory. Two hearts so united in suffering, two lives so interwoven in love, could not be kept apart. Love is only satisfied with presence. As it had behoved the Son to suffer and so enter into glory so it was right that she who had suffered should also enter into her glory. She who had so closely shared in the ending of the exile of God's people should not herself have to endure exile. Mary's longing to be united with her Son was matched by his desire to have her with him. Jesus had shown his love of his disciples by making them to be with him; he would give his final proof of his love of his Mother by making her also to be with him. So she set out on her final pilgrimage of faith to receive her eternal reward. The King desired her beauty and so she must hasten to his presence.

The Immaculate Virgin never knew the contagion of sin and it seemed proper that her body should not know the decay which is a consequence of sin. The Church's Tradition has preferred to think of her departure from this life as a transition through sleep rather than through death. St John Damascene, the great lover of her

Assumption, used all his mastery of imagery to describe it. 'God made her the beauteous treasure-house of all his riches . . . this Day the Treasure of Life is veiled in life-giving death. How could she who truly brought life to all become subject to death?'

Leaning on her Beloved

'Who is that coming up from the wilderness leaning upon her beloved?' (Cant 8, 5). Up out of the lowlands of this world Mary came, and it was fitting that she should lean on her beloved, for had he not willed to lean on her, supported by her strong and tender arms? Now she could lean on the strong arm of her Son, strong in all the power of his Resurrection. Her Assumption has aptly been described by Pope John Paul II as 'the special fruit of his Resurrection'. She who had come forth as the morning rising now went home in the splendid morning of her eternal glory.

When the Ark of the Covenant had crossed the threshold at the end of its triumphal journey there was a great shout of exultation. Now the new Ark of the Covenant was greeted by all the choirs of angels as she crossed the threshold to enter the eternal City of God. All the mysteries of her life, Annunciation, Visitation, Calvary, coalesced in this moment. The Lord who is mighty did the final great thing for her. Her Magnificat was now complete, or, rather it took on a new solemnity, becoming her song for eternity. Her Son could now address the whole family of the redeemed with a cry of joy, 'Behold your Mother'.

Ascending into heaven Jesus drew human hearts with him and he gave to the whole living of the christian life an upward impulse. He is always summoning us to the feast. The first to respond to that invitation was Mary, who came adorned as a bride to the wedding feast, radiant in beauty, robed in gold of Ophir.

During the earthly life of her Son hers was a life of intense activity as she served the mystery of salvation. Her mission continues. Just as her Son is ever making intercession to his Father for us, so also is his Mother pleading for us.

Mary Remembers

When Esther was chosen by the king to reign beside him, the people cried out, 'Remembering the days of your lowliness . . . beseech the Lord and speak to the king concerning us and deliver us from death' (Esther 4, 8). Mary, the new Esther, never ceases to speak for us to the king. The Lord remembers his mercy and she, who is the perfect reflection of her Son, keeps vividly in her mind and before us, his tender mercies. Her heart throbs with the same beat as the Heart of Jesus which is the fountain of mercy. Her memory is vivid and unfailing. Can a woman forget her child so as not to remember the son of her womb? Could Mary ever forget the Son of her womb? Neither can she forget the countless children born on Calvary from the Heart of her Son, and given into her keeping.

She remembers his mercy; she salutes that mercy from generation to generation; and it is her mission, as Mother of Mercy, to meet our deepest need by bringing us the full riches of his saving love. She remains a sign in the heavens of the eternal love of a merciful God who, through her, remains close to his people on their pilgrim journey. She exercises her queenship through her constant care of all her subjects, of the least as of the greatest. In the days of her lowliness, when she walked this earth, she had tasted all the joys and sorrows, the fears and heartbreaks, that are the history of any human life.

Sign of Hope

In the darkest perils in the life of the Church, and in our personal lives, the Queen of heaven shines through the darkness. In the dream of Mardocai, which introduces the Book of Esther, he relates how in response to the cry of the people in a day of 'darkness and gloom, tribulation and distress', they cried to God. 'And from their cry, as though from a tiny spring, there came a great river with abundant water, the light came and the sun rose and the lowly were exalted' (Esther 11, 8, 10). Using this theme, St Bonaventure builds a beautiful reflection on the Assumption. "Mary the Queen is also the distributor of grace. This is indicated in the Book of Esther, 'the little spring which grew into a river and was turned into the light and into the sun'. The Virgin Mother, under the type of Esther, is compared to the outpouring of a spring and of light". In the glory of the Assumption she is the perfect model of action and contemplation. The humble maiden of Nazareth has grown to full stature; the little spring has grown into a river. Mary is ever active, bringing to God's people the inexhaustible riches of salvation that flow like a great stream from the pierced side of her Son.

Side by side with her intense activity she is also in repose. Under the splendid light of glory her loving gaze ever feasts on the unutterable beauty of the inner life of the most Holy Trinity.

In 1950 Pope Pius XII proclaimed the dogma of Mary's Assumption. It was a moment when men's hearts were sickened by the scourge of a world war, the nausea of atomic destruction, the horror of concentration camps. Human eyes needed to be lifted up from the spectacle of smoking ruins to a new vision; and the vision he presented was Mary in all the freshness and beauty of her Assumption. It was enough to re-awaken a sense of wonder. The vision of Mary in glory met a deep human need in that moment. She lifted human hearts out of the wasteland of despair, and, as she had so often done before, she proved her nearness to her children in moments of greatest anguish and thus rekindled christian hopes.

Each of us needs a new vision; we need the mystery of Mary's Assumption to lift our eyes beyond earthly horizons. The grace of her Assumption is to make us more keenly aware that here we live in a world of shadows, that the great realities lie ahead, so that, like Bernadette of Lourdes, we live in a state of longing for our native air, the air of heaven.

Mary, assumed into heaven, beckons us away, and helps us to set our sights on the land of our dreams.

26 Mantling the Globe

When the wine failed, the mother of Jesus said to him, "They have no wine." And Jesus said to her, "O woman, what have you to do with me? My hour has not yet come."

His mother said to the servants, "Do whatever he tells you."

This, the first of his signs, Jesus did at Cana in Galilee, and manifested his glory; and his disciples believed in him.

John 2, 3-5, 11.

MARY is the universal mother. She folds the whole human family in her embrace. Her maternal gaze crosses the centuries. She belongs to every moment of history. Jesus Christ, 'yesterday and today and for ever' (Heb 13, 8), living on in his Mystical Body, the Church, belongs to the *now* of every person. Mary, Mother of the Church, brings the Church, with the riches of the grace of salvation into the possession of every person.

She is the sign appearing in the heavens; but she is not merely a spectator of our lives, looking on us from a distance. She walks our pilgrim road with us. She is 'the sure hope and comfort of the people of God on their pilgrimage' *(Vat. II, The Church).*

'Today, if you would listen to his voice' (Ps 95, 7). Mary was the one creature who listened to his voice in an eternal today. The pleadings and longings of God's people find an echo in her heart. Just as Esther did not close her ears to the needs of her people when she was raised up to her new status beside the king, so Mary, now enthroned beside the King, is ever active with her intercession for everyone of us, her children.

As she had listened to a world longing for a Saviour, she keeps her ears attentive to the prayers of a world redeemed.

The Church carries the Cross of Christ through the centuries. She presents the Word which is fresh as when it first was spoken, and is relevant to every circumstance and problem of our time. Mary, who stood by the Cross, walks with the Church at every moment. She teaches the Church how to listen to our world. She brings to our world the compassion which she shares with her Son for the poor and little ones of Israel. Therefore the Church, in all truth, can claim that 'the joys and hopes, the griefs and anguish of the men of our times, especially those who are poor and afflicted in any way, are the joys and hopes, the griefs and anguish of the followers of Christ as well' *(Vat. 11 The Church in the modern world.)*

Mary is a model in listening. She has a mother's sensitive ear for the cry of her children; she hears the cry of hunger, the cry of sorrow. She is attentive to the whispered pleadings coming through a dark night of pain. Her song of joy mingles with the laughter of childhood. She keeps a ceaseless vigil. "He slumbers not neither does he sleep who watches over Israel" (Ps 121, 4). Mary is the mother who, through the day and through the long night hours, watches with love over the new Israel. She is rightly saluted as Comforter of the Afflicted.

Signs of the Times

The pilgrim road takes the people of our century along terrain not easy to traverse; each step brings new hazards; dark clouds of false teaching often obscure the light. We need guidance; we need signposts for eternity in order to reach our goal. Mary, Seat of Wisdom, gives us guidance; Mary, Morning Star, gives direction. She helps the Church 'to read the signs of the times and to interpret them in the light of the gospel'.

Our world suffers from a blurred vision of the truth. A people, walking in semi-darkness, is in need of a great light. Mary, the woman clothed in the sun, is a sign appearing in the heavens; she is a sign for all of us. In the resplendent beauty of her sinlessness she mirrors the central truths of our faith, the redeeming love of her son, the malice of sin, our need of forgiveness which, in our day, have often been challenged or bypassed.

Pope Paul VI

In his Apostolic Exhortation, *Marialis Cultus,* Pope Paul VI beautifully describes the exercise of

Mary's motherhood related to these great truths.

The action of the Church in the world can be likened to an extension of Mary's concern. "The active love she showed at Nazareth, in the house of Elizabeth, at Cana and on Golgotha, finds its extension in the Church's maternal concern that all men should come to the knowledge of the truth" (cf. 1 Tim 2, 4). He gives a masterly analysis of the many symptoms of malaise which are a sign of our times, and how Mary comes to our aid to combat them. 'Modern man, so often torn between anguish and hope, defeated by the sense of his own limitations and assailed by limitless aspirations, troubled in his mind and divided in his heart . . .'

There is the anguish caused by violence, by the exploiting of the weak, and by the wreckage of God's loving plan at the hands of a permissive society. we are lured to expect a better world by the material enticements of consumerism. A world, ever promising but never fulfilling, advertises itself to us as a Utopia of our dreams. So often our minds are not at rest; we can be tempted to question the deepest realities of our faith, finding ourselves caught up in the fashion of discussion which never brings decisions.

The handmaid of the Lord had limitless aspirations, but they were centred on him. Her heart was never divided; she was always at rest. She showed the victory of hope over anguish. Even in her deepest suffering, there was never anguish; she could rejoice in God her Saviour.

'Man is oppressed by loneliness while yearning for fellowship.' A paradox of our times is that while so many media of communication and social groups seem to be drawing people together, yet so many, both young and old, are oppressed by a deep loneliness. Mary has removed the source of

158

all our loneliness. Having given her Son the comfort of her companionship in his hour of abandonment on the Cross, she now stands close to us in our darkest moments, and with the true instinct of a mother she knows when our need of a mother's presence is greatest.

Boredom

'Man is a prey to boredom and disgust.' Boredom has become a kind of fashion, and is often presented as a way of expressing maturity. But it takes its toll; it dries up the freshness of our love for Christ; it brings a feeling of fatigue with prayer; it seeps its way into our approach to the Holy Eucharist. When God's people were given the most wonderful sign of his love in his providing manna from heaven every day, at a certain moment they lost their sense of wonder; and with that went their sense of appreciation and thanks. 'We are tired of this worthless food,' (Num 21, 5) they cried out.

Mary shows us how to overcome boredom by refreshing our sense of wonder. She never lost her wonderment. She is always seeing her Child for the first time. She brings her Son across the threshold of our generation, singing her magnificat, which remains fresh and pure as when, for the first time, she rejoiced in God her Saviour. There is no better antidote to boredom than to enter into the mood of that canticle and sing it with her who was too enraptured by the great things of God to become a victim of boredom.

Message of Springtime

Mary brings to the world a message of springtime; it is a message of immense hope, assuring us that, 'the winter is past . . . the flowers appear on the earth.' (Cant 2, 11, 12). This day a Saviour is being born for us, for the mystery of the Incarnation is always new. A young mother, radiant with the beauty of another world, presents her Son, source of life and joy and peace, to a jaded world that has lost its dreams. We stand in awe before the tenderness of her care and love of him. Because she is the mother who cares also for us, she teaches us how to sing a new song to him; she opens our hearts to his love. As the handmaid of the Lord she served his needs — so also does she care for us, sheltering us from the hazards of the road, lifting our eyes towards eternal horizons.

Whether we gaze on the Mother and the Child in the darkness of the stable, or see her as the Queen beside the King, her beauty entrances us, and we are certain that her love enfolds us, and that, in her maternal care, she will be with us until we reach home. A truth that can transform our lives is this: the same strong arms that sheltered the Son of God hold us also in a tender embrace.

The poem of Caryll Houselander puts it in lovely words:

The circle of a girl's arms
has changed the world –
the round and sorrowful world –
to a cradle for God.'

27 The Pilgrim Church

So those who received his word were
baptized, and there were added that day
about three thousand souls. And they
devoted themselves to the apostles'
teaching and fellowship, to the breaking
of bread and the prayers.

And the Lord added to their number
day by day those who were being saved.

Acts 2, 41, 42, 47.

AFTER the day of Pentecost the Church set out on her road, bearing the Cross of Christ through the centuries, filling the world with the splendid light of the risen Lord. "For us and for our salvation." The loving plan of God for our salvation, which began with the Incarnation, yielded its fruits from the very first moments of the Church's life, in the creation of a new people walking in newness of life.

The apostles carried the precious treasure of the Faith in earthen vessels, but they were worthy of their sacred task, for they were no longer subject to the fragility of their condition as they had been before the coming of the Holy Spirit. They pressed forward with the irresistible urge to hand on the Good News. "We cannot keep silent about the things we have heard and seen" (Acts 4, 20). Once, Peter, in a moment of false bravery, had protested "I will go and die with you" (Jn 13, 37). But it needed the strengthening of the Holy Spirit to make this protestation a reality.

They had been witnesses of the progressive revelation of his saving love, and with hearts full of the infectious joy of his paschal victory they issued a universal call to salvation; and their preaching created a people. It is a fascinating story — the formation of little christian communities responding to the Holy Spirit, who gathered them together making them one in heart and mind, forming them into a kind of permanent liturgy, in their unceasing coming together for songs and canticles and in the breaking of bread and of prayers.

Few to Many

There is no proportion between the fewness of the preachers, the littleness of the first christian communities, and the mighty works they proclaimed and achieved. At the beginning of Redemption, God had used the littleness of Mary to do great things through her. As the fruits of Redemption were being dispensed to the Church, the Lord looked on his apostolic servants in their nothingness.

Cardinal Newman has a phrase: "Grace ever works through the few." The apostolic sowers of the seed were few. It seemed, in the words of a second century writer, "a grain of wheat scattered on the mountainside," here and there taking root, seemingly at random. Lydia, "a seller of purple goods . . . The Lord opened her heart . . . she was baptized, with her household" (Acts 16, 14, 15). The simple question of Paul's jailer, "What must I do to be saved?", was enough to indicate his readiness to accept the Faith. "He was baptized at once, with all his family" (Acts 16, 31, 34).

A notable feature of the infant Church was the intimate bond of affection and obedience between the apostles and the young christian communities. There was the childlike openness to their message, the readiness to heed reproofs or warnings against abuses or dangers that often menaced their life. There was the interaction of prayer and praise. Paul was constantly praising the faith of the people, and thanking God for their faithfulness. When Peter was in prison, "earnest prayer for him was made to God by the Church" (Acts 12, 5). When Paul was leaving Ephesus the people accompanied him to the shore to say farewell. "He knelt down and prayed with them all. And they all wept and embraced Paul and kissed him" (Acts 20, 37). In his closing address in his letter to the Romans, he lists by name, in a kind of roll-call of honour, twenty-eight fellow workers, whose conversion and enduring work he greeted with thanks and prayers.

Yesterday and Today

Jesus Christ is of yesterday and today. The yesterday of the infant Church and the today of the Church of our century have the same features.

We, the pilgrim people, walk the same road, often beset by unseen hazards, often weary from the journey, and yet ever straining forward, buoyed up by the hope that does not disappoint us.

The Second Vatican Council showed the Church looking inwards on her own nature, and rediscovering for the people of the twentieth century her function and beauty and inner vitalities, together with her understanding and sensitivity to the problems of our world. "The Church, 'like a pilgrim in a foreign land presses forward amid the persecutions of the world and the consolations of God', announcing the cross and death of the Lord until he comes (cf. 1, Cor 11, 26). By the power of the risen Lord, she is given strength to overcome patiently and lovingly the afflictions and hardships which assail her from within and without, and to show forth in the world the mystery of the Lord in a faithful though shadowed way, until at last it will be revealed in total splendour."

The Council reflected on the essential purpose of the Church to bring all men into a living union with Christ and with one another. Thus, as the sacraments bring divine life and are the source of constant growth of that life, so the Church may be called "a kind of sacrament or a sign of intimate union with God and of the unity of all mankind."

Beneath that strong light there appear ever new vistas of her beauty and holiness that open out before our vision. And because the mystery of the Incarnation is always new, so the mystery of the saving action and presence of the Incarnate Word in the Church is always new, with a message that is contemporary in every age. Pope Paul VI aptly described the unceasing quest of the Church for an ever deeper knowledge of herself. "The

164

Church is a mystery. It is a reality imbued with the hidden presence of God. It lies, therefore, within the very nature of the Church to be always open to new and greater exploration."

The Three Metaphors

We can return, as did Vatican II, to dwell on the great metaphors by which the Church is described in Holy Scripture — The Building, the Body, the Bride. Each presents the idea of constant activity — every member of the Church is meant to share in the process of growth which will go on till the Church reaches her final destiny.

"You are God's building" (1, Cor 3, 8), the building founded on the secure foundation which is Jesus Christ. Each of us is one of the 'living stones' with our own personal contribution to strengthen God's holy temple.

"You are the body of Christ and individually members of it" (1, Cor 12, 27). As members, we receive life, and, as well, we are contributing to the building up of the Body of Christ.

The third of the great metaphors describes the Church as a Bride, the spotless spouse of the spotless Lamb "whom Christ loved and delivered himself up for her" (Eph 5, 26).

Those vivid descriptions of the Church derive from the risen life of Jesus. "Destroy this temple." But in three days he rebuilt it, and the victory of his resurrection became the foundation of the resurrection Church. He allowed his Body to be drained of life, but the water and the blood that flowed from his side became the fountain of life; his blood did not flow in vain, it became the life-blood of his Body, the Church. When man had disfigured his Body and 'there was no beauty in him,' God raised him from the dead, and embellished him with the resurrection radiance which he lavished on his Bride, the Church

It is for each of us to try to penetrate ever more deeply into the inner beauty of the great truths which they light up, and which make us more aware of our sublime status as members of God's holy people. They are each a revelation that tells us how we have been destined in love, how, through the personal love of Jesus for us, which surpasses all understanding, we are being moulded into his likeness.

When the shadows have passed, then we shall go forward to meet the Bridegroom in the light of everlasting day.